WITHDRAWN

D0067879

A PASSION FOR FILMS

ALSO BY RICHARD ROUD

MAX OPHÜLS: AN INDEX

JEAN-LUC GODARD

JEAN-MARIE STRAUB

CINEMA: A CRITICAL DICTIONARY (Editor)

PHOTOGRAPH OPPOSITE,
Henri Langlois in front of a maquette from
Georges Méliès's *Conquest of the Pole.*
© *1982 by Pierre Boulat, Cosmos*

A PASSION FOR FILMS
Henri Langlois and the
Cinémathèque Française

Richard Roud

THE JOHNS HOPKINS UNIVERSITY PRESS
BALTIMORE AND LONDON

TO MARY MEERSON

Hardcover edition originally published by The Viking Press, New York, 1983
Copyright © 1983 by Richard Roud
All rights reserved
Johns Hopkins Paperbacks edition, 1999
Printed in the United States of America on acid-free paper
9 8 7 6 5 4 3 2 1

The Johns Hopkins University Press
2715 North Charles Street
Baltimore, Maryland 21218-4363
www.press.jhu.edu

Library of Congress Cataloging-in-Publication Data

Roud, Richard.
    A passion for films : Henri Langlois and the Cinémathèque française /
Richard Roud. — Johns Hopkins paperbacks ed.
        p.   cm.
    Originally published : New York : Viking Press, c1983.
    Includes bibliographical references and index.
    ISBN 0-8018-6206-X (alk. paper)
    1. Langlois, Henri, 1914–1977. 2. Cinémathèque française. I. Title.
PN1998.3.L38R68   1999
026´.79143´092—dc21
[B]
                                                                    99-14614
                                                                    CIP

A catalog record for this book is available from the British Library.

Foreword by François Truffaut

L ike the play that Alexandre Dumas devoted to the great
English actor Edmund Kean, Richard Roud's book could
be subtitled "Disorder and Genius."

Several months after the death of the founder of the Cinémathèque Française, a *cinéphile* from San Francisco said to
me: "Really, the French have no gift for biography. If Henri
Langlois had been American, there would already be three
works about him in the bookstore windows."

This remark is as valid for literature as it is for cinema. If
one wants to know the life of Marcel Proust, one has to read

the biography by the English writer George D. Painter. To learn who Jean Cocteau was, one must go to the book by the American Francis Steegmuller.

French writers all too often come from the universities and all too rarely from journalism, and they prefer to publish theses that will get them promotions in the academic hierarchy rather than to apply themselves to factual research aimed at reconstituting a life story. And yet nothing dates more quickly than theoretical works on art, doubtless because they are constructed according to methods elaborated from ideologies that spring up one after another, contradict each other, and replace each other in the way that, as the French say, one nail drives out another. Therefore, the interest of such works is as ephemeral, and almost as seasonal, as the haute-couture changes of skirt lengths.

That is why all those who were close to Henri Langlois, who loved him or were at odds with him, will be grateful to Richard Roud for having played the investigator rather than the professor, for having put on the gumshoes of Philip Marlowe rather than the spats of a literary theorist like the now largely forgotten Albert Thibaudet. For Roud has brought to life a man as picturesque and as contradictory as a Dickens character, a man who gave his friendship sparingly, and who could withdraw it on a caprice, a suspicion, or an "intuition."

In *Mr. Arkadin*, the title character, played by Orson Welles, recounts a dream he has had: wandering through a cemetery, he noticed that all the tombstones had pairs of dates very close to each other: 1919–1925 or 1907–1913. He asked the cemetery watchman, "Do the people in this country all die young?" "No," answered the watchman, "these dates indicate the length of time that a friendship lasted."

And indeed, even when friendship has been durable and has never been betrayed, we are able to follow those we love

Foreword

only for a moment of their lives, only for a part of their paths through life. Biographers sometimes tell us more about our-selves than about the people who are their subjects; the read-ing of biographies fascinates us more and more as we get older. Although I was very close to André Bazin for the last ten years of his life (he died when he was forty), I had to wait for Dudley Andrew's biography to learn about his first thirty years.

Thanks to Richard Roud—who represents for many Euro-pean filmmakers (as for me) the "American friend," even if his friend Langlois persistently pretended to think he was a British subject—a veil, nay, a thick and well-kept-up curtain of mystery rises to reveal to us the founder of the Ciné-mathèque Française, a man who was both unassuming and ex-travagant, a fabulous man, an obsessed man, a man animated by an *idée fixe*, a haunted man.

Like all "haunted" men, Henri Langlois divided the world, people, and events into two camps: (1) what was good for the Cinémathèque Française and (2) what was bad for it. Even if you had been friends with him for a decade, he never wasted time asking how you were, or how your family was getting along, because the very notions of health and family could be related only to the health of the Cinémathèque, the family of the Cinémathèque. This didn't stop him from proving a warm friend, on condition that you agreed to jump onto the moving train of his conversation, which was, more exactly, a mono-logue revolving around a conspiracy, about which he didn't care if you understood the particulars. For example: "Hello, Henri, how goes it?" "Very badly. The rue de Valois [the Ministry of Culture] wants to cancel the March 17th General Assembly because of the proxies, but I told Comptroller Pas-quet that if the Ministry didn't take into account the July 23rd resolutions, I would close the rue de Courcelles building and would convene the members of the subcommission to read them the Novak report prepared for FIAF as a result of resolution 35B of the Locarno Manifesto, and I then told Viktor to tell Bascafe that they weren't going to get away with doing to me on March 11th what they did last April 29th."

One got used to listening to him without understanding a word, not asking any questions, like someone who can't read music confronted with a musical score. One felt great sympathy for this paranoid volubility, those conspiratorial glances. We all joked about it among ourselves until that moment in February 1968 when it became clear that it all had a foundation in fact.

Nineteen sixty-eight! For ten years France had been governed by an authoritarian and anachronistic old man. That state of things, which seemed natural to those who had accepted or undergone the Marshal Pétain regime, was unbearable for the younger French, who had been born after the war. In the France of General de Gaulle, you had to wait until you were twenty-one to vote, whereas the whole country was becoming Americanized, and a 19-year-old singer called Johnny Halliday had become a national glory before he was called up for military service.

It wasn't until the de Gaulle government tried to eliminate Henri Langlois from the Cinémathèque he had created that the wind of disobedience rose, and the streets of Paris were filled with protesters. With the passing of time, it seems obvious that the demonstrations for Langlois were to the events of May '68 what the trailer is to the feature film coming soon.

This is so true that after the first demonstration, on February 14, 1968, which gathered only the "Children of the Cinémathèque," we began to see our embattled troops augmented, in the demonstrations that followed, by unknown faces, those of Maoist and anarchist students, some of whom were shortly

Foreword

to become famous. Their leaders fraternized with us, observed us, and then began to criticize our political amateurism. I can still see Daniel Cohn-Bendit perched on a lamp post in the rue de Courcelles, reproaching us for having dispersed too soon—before having rescued one of our "comrades" who had spat in the face of a member of the C.R.S.* and was being held in a paddywagon.

The Cinémathèque *affaire* effectively had made militants of us all, but not necessarily political militants. As protests against Langlois's eviction came in from every corner of the globe, I was not surprised one morning to get a phone call from London. It was from Vanessa Redgrave, who invited me to come the following Sunday for a mass demonstration that would parade through central London. I agreed immediately. Then she gave me the details: "The parade will start at 11 a.m. from Hyde Park. We've decided to each wear a handkerchief around our foreheads." I interrupted her: "What an odd idea. I wonder what Langlois will think of it." "Who's talking about Langlois? I'm inviting you to an anti-Vietnam war demonstration." As you may have guessed, the cause didn't seem to me to be worth a one-day round trip to London, and I declined the invitation in order to plunge back into the activities of the "Cinémathèque Defense Committee."

Langlois was no more political than we were, and while the "Children of the Cinémathèque" were getting themselves hit on the head by the C.R.S. in the streets of Paris, Henri was spending his time in his apartment on the rue Gazan playing solitaire, or arranging to be driven to fortune-tellers, the only ones, according to him, who were capable of predicting the fate of the Cinémathèque.

However, it would be a mistake to believe that Langlois

* The equivalent of the National Guard.—R. R.

was passively accepting the situation. He was encouraged in his intransigence by Mary Meerson, who was, if that were possible, even more determined than he not to give in. For many years she had prophesied the approach of dark clouds over the Cinémathèque; it was she who had divined the maneuvers of those who envied Langlois and coveted the Cinémathèque; and her prophecies had been more than fulfilled. He had the diabolical cleverness to keep absolutely silent during the whole of the *affaire*, not to make a single declaration to the press nor to initiate a single official act; however, he knew exactly how to maneuver and inspire the troops of followers who had spontaneously put themselves at his disposition—through the association we had immediately created under the name of "The Cinémathèque Française Defense Committee."

The struggle was carried out on all fronts, in the streets, in offices, on the phone. We inundated the newspapers with our articles and *communiqués*. They were at first favorable to our cause, but then became more and more intimidated by the government. Several hundred directors, from Chaplin to Kurosawa, from Satyajit Ray to Rossellini, sent telegrams to *Cahiers du Cinéma*—very active in this struggle—threatening to withdraw their films from a Cinémathèque deprived of Langlois. Finally, as Richard Roud explains so well, the government had to give in, not only because of the pressure of the *cinéphiles* but also thanks to the effective action behind the scenes of some powerful men, the most important of whom was Jean Riboud, chief operating officer of the multinational Schlumberger company and a friend of the arts. Once Langlois was reinstated, we could get some sleep again and go back to our own work.

We all have very passionate memories of this period of devotion to a cause, of personal sacrifices, and of that absence of any doubt which characterizes commitment when it is per-

Foreword

sonally felt. To be completely frank, I would say that we may have been on occasion preemptory, hateful, and slightly terroristic; militancy often carries with it, consciously or not, a good dose of bad faith. So I understood only *a posteriori* that it took a certain amount of courage for Langlois's adversaries to express and maintain their position during this period. I'm not talking now of those who were plotting to get his job, but of a minority of filmmakers, historians, or collectors who felt that Langlois's faults were greater than his qualities, and that more rigor was henceforth necessary to preserve films. That, for example, was the point of view of the excellent director Roger Leenhardt.

In spite of this shadow on the picture, the battle of the Cinémathèque counted also because it marked the first—and probably the last—reunion of those enthusiastic young people who, ten years earlier, had given birth, in an atmosphere of rather exceptional camaraderie, to the "new wave." But the directors of the preceding generation—men like Jean Renoir, Marcel Carné, and Henri-Georges Clouzot—also joined forces with the "New Wave," and, reconciled with them, fought at their side. In this struggle, French cinema presented a united front against the enemy, against the Ministry of Finance and the Ministry of Culture. What was called the "Cinémathèque affair," those three months of crisis at the beginning of 1968, would justify a whole book, but the long chapter that Richard Roud devotes to it is absolutely accurate.

If May 1968 gave the impression that France had become an arena in which General de Gaulle was battling the anarchist Daniel Cohn-Bendit, three months earlier we had the impression that the bout was being fought between de Gaulle and Langlois. And yet it does not seem improper to sketch out a comparison between the two men.

Just as the general intimately identified himself with

France, so Langlois identified himself with the Cinémathèque. The feeling of his own importance had led de Gaulle
to take on Churchill, Roosevelt, and Stalin; Langlois, for the
same reasons, had taken on the directors of the other film libraries of the world. In excluding himself from the powerful
Federation of Film Archives, Langlois imitated de Gaulle
leaving NATO or treating the U.N. as a "gadget." And
again, like de Gaulle, Langlois accepted as his friends or collaborators only "unconditionals." Anti-communist, anti-
socialist, Langlois was certainly in no way Gaullist, but he
was profoundly Gaullian in his style.

The Cinémathèque crisis was born of the hostility of certain civil servants to Langlois himself. Behind their peevish-
ness, there was the unavowed hatred of poetry, or, more
precisely, the hatred of poetic behavior, within an institution
where the administrative sector was taking on too much power. Henri Langlois was not a *filmmaker** but a *screening-
maker.** Buying, exchanging, and saving films is perhaps not
a profession but the exercising of a passion. Langlois was perhaps the most gifted of film lovers. I don't know whether or
not in his heart of hearts Langlois—whose life was devoted to
films—regretted that he had never made any himself, but I
am convinced that a filmmaker, talented or not, would never
have been able to create and keep alive the Cinémathèque for
the very good reason that an artist, even one who is very
open, curious, tolerant, and well-meaning, cannot really understand or accept the work of his colleagues.

In French prewar cinema, all the important directors, from
Renoir to Buñuel, sneered at the lyricism and grandiloquence
of Abel Gance. René Clair's contempt for Pagnol at the beginning of the thirties was echoed by Welles's, later on, for

* In English in the original.—R. R.

Foreword

Rossellini. Hitchcock saw in the work of his colleagues who had not made silent films only "photographs of people talking." Robert Bresson, at the time he made his own *Jeanne d'Arc*, said when asked about Carl Dreyer's film on the same subject that all he could see in it was a festival of grimacing faces.

These examples are neither exceptional nor scandalous; they are logical and normal. Only the lovers of an art can respond to all its aspects, can enjoy the whole range, the spread of the fan. When one becomes a filmmaker after having been a *cinéphile*, the number of specific problems to be solved makes one forget one's admirations and obliges one to create all sorts of unwritten personal laws, which soon become so constraining that the filmmaker loses all freshness when confronted with the work of colleagues who have forged other laws and carried them through.

That is why, contrary to a widespread notion, the presence of a filmmaker is not at all desirable on a jury, or a selection committee, and even less so at the head of a festival or an archive. If, in spite of his capriciousness, Langlois was the best Cinémathèque director, it was because, ever since his early days as a collector, he refused to select, to choose; and because he decided that every piece of exposed film should be preserved, precisely to save it from the capriciousness of judgments conditioned by the fashions of a period. Richard Roud expresses this clearly in his description of Langlois defending the films of Louis Feuillade against his filmmaking contemporaries, and, closer to our own time, defending the films of Howard Hawks, so disdained by American intellectuals. Langlois loved the cinema sensually.

When a former friend or collaborator of Langlois's stopped giving him his "unconditional" support, Henri, incapable of accepting the slightest reserve in a friendship or a collaboration, immediately classified that person among his enemies, although he continued to speak of him without hatred, almost always offering the same explanation: "This quarrel is absolutely normal; X saw me as a father and now he feels the need to kill his father-figure." It was in these terms that Langlois must have spoken of me when, in 1973, I quietly left the administrative council of the Cinémathèque. If I had been disappointed by what the Cinémathèque had become in the years after 1968, this disappointment did not affect my friendship with Langlois. So it was not without a certain sadness that I noticed a cooling of our relationship at the time when his health was deteriorating.

A happy chance was to allow me to meet Henri for the last time in a warm and friendly atmosphere. Lotte Eisner's nieces gave a party to celebrate the eightieth birthday of their adorable aunt one summer's night in 1976 in Neuilly. Most of Paris was away on vacation, so we made up an intimate group. The weather was splendid, and the windows opened out onto the most beautiful trees in the Bois de Boulogne. The nieces were very gracious: Pierre Prévert was making puns; Lotte Eisner was glowing with pleasure; and we were all eating *petits fours* and drinking champagne. More out of breath than ever, Langlois was *not* talking only of the Cinémathèque but spoke about his own health, which was even more upsetting to his friends than to himself. A dentist had suggested pulling out all his teeth; a doctor wanted to send him to a spa; a surgeon thought he ought to have an operation. Langlois rejected all these suggestions and talked about the doctors the way he used to talk about the state financial comptrollers. But all this didn't prevent us from smiling and laughing. For once, a meeting indirectly linked to the Cinémathèque was held in a joyful, straightforward atmosphere: no conspiracies, no mistrust, no suspicions—simply the moving celebration of the

Foreword

birthday of an angel, for Lotte Eisner was indeed the angel of
the Cinémathèque, just as Mary Meerson was its Beatrice.

Henri was eighteen years younger than Lotte Eisner, but he
was to disappear six months later. Did he die of sadness or of
illness? I believe in the first hypothesis. His heart was bruised
by a feeling of powerlessness: what a man alone has created he
cannot preserve.

October 1982

Translated by R. R.

Acknowledgments

My thanks to:

Margareta Akermark,
Kenneth Anger,
Jean-Michel Arnold,
Bernardo Bertolucci,
Agnes Bleier-Brody,
Marcie Bloom,
Sallie Wilensky Blumenthal,
Pierre-André Boutang
Pierre Braunberger,

Louise Brooks,
Freddy Buache,
James Card,
Carlos Clarens,
Sue Craig,
João Benard Da Costa,
Jean Diard,
Yvonne Dornès,
Lotte Eisner,

Acknowledgments

Marie Epstein,
Enrico Fulchignioni,
Georges Franju,
John Gillett,
Jean-Luc Godard,
Georges Goldfayn,
Harvey Gram,
S. Frederick Gronich,
Roberto Guerra,
Gillian Hartnoll,
Anne Head,
Annabel Herbout,
Eila Hershon,
Françoise Jaubert,
Thomas Johnston,
Kashiko Kawakita,
Edwin Kennebeck,
Arthur Knight,
Georges Langlois,
Jacques Ledoux,
Lucie Lichtig,
Renée Lichtig,
Joseph Losey,
Serge Losique,
Tom Luddy,
Sybille de Luze,
Bernard Martinand,
Corine McMullen,
David Meeker,

Harry Meerson,
Mary Meerson,
Dominique de Menil,
Simon Mizrahi,
Jean-Yves Mock,
Enno Patalas,
Pierre Prévert,
Derek Prouse,
German Puig,
Karel Reisz,
Sheldon Renan,
Alain Resnais,
Jean Riboud,
Jacques Rivette,
David Robinson,
Raymond Rohauer,
Jean Rouch,
Marku Salmi,
Helen G. Scott,
Peter Seward,
Michelle Snapes,
Eugene Stavis,
Elliott Stein,
Simone Swann,
André Thirifays,
Alexandre Trauner,
François Truffaut,
Peter Willits, and
Basil Wright.

Contents

Contents

Photographs follow page 128.

Just one thing makes [Antoinette Sibley] a little sad. Recently she went to lecture to the Royal Ballet School students, and thought she'd take some films along, as many of them would be too young to have seen her dance. She found that, except for two early fragments, there was nothing. The BBC had wiped her off its tapes, and the Royal Ballet School had somehow missed video-taping her dancing, even in the ballets she created. It was a bad blow. "I'd thought: Well, I've had a wonderful career; I can't add to it, but at least it's there—what I've done I've done. Then to find nothing. It was a horror story, worse than stopping dancing. It was as if I'd never been there." —*The Observer* (London), March 29, 1981

Introduction

At the end of February 1968, President de Gaulle suppos-
edly asked his staff, "Who *is* this Henri Langlois?" The
simple answer he probably knew: Henri Langlois was the cofounder of the Cinémathèque Française (*cinémathèque* means
film library, just as discothèque originally meant record library); for over thirty years he had officially been its secretary-
general and in fact the man who ran it.

But the simple answer would not have been enough for de
Gaulle, because it could not explain why the dismissal of
Langlois by André Malraux, the Minister of Culture, had

Introduction

brought the whole French film industry out onto the streets. It would not explain why the world's most famous and important film directors, actors, actresses, and technicians were sending telegrams of support to Langlois and telegrams to the new administrator of the Cinémathèque refusing him the right to show their films, and thus forcing him to suspend operations. How could the dismissal of a minor official—a librarian—account for mass meetings, physical confrontations with the police, daily reports in the newspapers, and an almost general condemnation of the government?

Of course, de Gaulle was asking the wrong people. Lillian Gish would answer: "Of all the men I have ever met in the world, Henri Langlois is the most dedicated to the preservation of films. He has no money, he has very little power, and he comes from a small country, as the world goes. But he was a man of destiny, born to do one thing. Nothing in life means anything to Langlois but film and the preservation of films. I think he would die for the films he has collected."[1]

Jean Renoir could have told him: "We owe to Henri Langlois—and Mary Meerson—the development of a certain passion for films. . . . I'm sure many young people who know and are more or less interested in my work would have never heard of me without the Cinémathèque. This Cinémathèque is—perhaps I should use the word—the church for movies. It is the best school for young directors. All the good directors of the New Wave spent their young years at the Cinémathèque watching films to learn how to become a director by watching how the other films were directed." And Renoir could have added that one of his most famous films, Une Partie de Campagne (A Day in the Country), would not have come down to us had Langlois not saved the negative during the German Occupation.

For Alain Resnais, Langlois was "my idol. He made me

discover films I couldn't see elsewhere. Not just Feuillade, but Buñuel, Fritz Lang, the Russian classics, *Greed, Intolerance*." Bernardo Bertolucci put it more succinctly: "The only school for the cinema is to go to the cinema and not waste time studying theory in film schools. The best school of cinema in the world is the Cinémathèque in Paris. And the best professor is Henri Langlois." Wim Wenders also testified to the importance of the Cinémathèque. In a letter to Lotte Eisner, one of Langlois's colleagues and the world's greatest authority on German cinema, he wrote that when he went to Paris for the 1965–66 season it was the Cinémathèque that gave him his film education. For him, the Cinémathèque was not just a place where films were shown—it was rather that the cinema itself was present there. So although some people thought of Langlois, in Jean Cocteau's famous phrase, as "the old dragon who guards our treasures," for young filmmakers everywhere a winter at the Cinémathèque was the confirmation of a vocation (or indeed, as with Wenders, the origin of one). *

In an editorial in *Cahiers du Cinéma* (unsigned, but the editors included Godard, Rivette, and Truffaut), one could read, "Without Langlois there would be neither *Cahiers du Cinéma* nor New Wave."[2] Even André Malraux, nominally responsible for Langlois's dismissal, could have said that had it not been for Langlois, his own film *Espoir* would no longer exist. France's greatest directors, René Clair, Marcel L'Herbier, and, above all, Abel Gance, could have testified to the same: without Langlois, for example, Gance's *Napoléon* would not have survived and those triumphant screenings in 1981 would have been impossible.

Langlois had saved for posterity a number of important

---

*After Langlois's death, Wenders was to dedicate his film *The American Friend* to Langlois.

films, and he had formed a whole generation of filmmakers by showing them the masterpieces of the cinema. As he himself put it, in his inimitable English: "I have never said this movie is good, this movie is bad; they discover by themselves. I have not helped, I have not taught. I have put food on the table and they have taken the food and eaten, and then gone on to eat more and more food. All I give them is food, food, food, food. This is my work, to show films; to save and to show films, nothing more. Henri Langlois does not exist; only exists the Cinémathèque Française. . . . Not exist Henri Langlois, only exists the Cinémathèque Française."[3]

But there had to be more than that to make the protest against Langlois's dismissal a kind of dress rehearsal for the more spectacular demonstrations, the "events" of May 1968. As Jacques Doniol-Valcroze, director and editor of *Cahiers du Cinéma*, put it, "Only Langlois's personality could set off such a phenomenon of solidarity. The only excuse for the picturesque disorder of the Cinémathèque Française was the presence of Langlois's genius. He was one of the true creators of the French cinema. That's why we defended him blindly, in spite of everything."

"In spite of everything": what does that mean? As Simone Signoret said, "He's a little bit of a nut," or as Jeanne Moreau more tactfully expressed it, "Henri Langlois is an eternal child. . . . Like all people with a truly deep passion and truly fantastic enthusiasm, he acts like a child. François Truffaut told me, 'Langlois always travels with two plane tickets because he tends to lose one of them. . . .' He is so obsessed that he doesn't think of ordinary life. For Henri Langlois, films mean life . . . that's the way life is lived for him."

To quote Ingrid Bergman, "Henri Langlois has created a work of art. Like a painter creates a painting, a sculptor a sculpture, he has created a Cinémathèque." If one believes,

Introduction

as I do, that, for all its failings, the period of filmmaking usually called the New Wave—the progression of masterpieces
(and flops) that began in 1958—was a golden era for the cinema (perhaps its last golden era), we must accept the testimony of the creators and the audiences of the New Wave era
that they owe an incalculable debt to Henri Langlois.

Langlois was one of the world's great eccentrics—"the most
unforgettable character I ever met," to use the old *Reader's
Digest* phrase. But in spite of his eccentricity, or because of it,
he managed to achieve what Nicholas Ray called "perhaps
the most important individual effort ever accomplished in the
history of the cinema." In the words of Jean-Luc Godard,
Henri Langlois is "one of the greatest French film directors,
director and scriptwriter of a continuous film called the Cinémathèque Française." And the Cinémathèque, said Jacques
Rivette, "is both the Louvre and the Museum of Modern Art
of film as they should be, and not as they are. It is also the
Galerie Maeght and the Galerie Sonnabend. One could see
there successively at 6:30 p.m. Griffith's *Broken Blossoms* and
at 8:30 Andy Warhol's *The Chelsea Girls*. And it was fabulous
precisely because one could see Griffith and Warhol together
on the same night. Because it was then that one realized that
there are not two or three kinds of cinema, there is only one
cinema. It was the perpetual interaction of the present and
the past of the cinema that was so exciting."

In a sense, this book is an attempt to answer President de
Gaulle's question. It is not an easy task, because the life of
Langlois has gathered many legends around it. It is necessary
to puncture a few of them to understand where the true genius of Langlois lay. For example, the Cinémathèque Française was not, in spite of what was said and written in 1968
and has been repeated ever since, the first film archive in the
world. That honor must go to the Swedish Archive. The Cin-

Introduction

émathèque Française, in spite of all that has been said and written, is not the largest archive in the world. Langlois himself always said that East Berlin's was the biggest. "The biggest" is a fuzzy and relative concept in the archive world, because it all depends on how you count. Some archives count duplicates in their tallies; others don't. In fact, to this day nobody knows how many films there are in the Cinémathèque Française. But it doesn't matter; as Langlois himself said to me, "The secret of the Cinémathèque Française is not the 50,000 films, nor is it that it shows seven films a day. That's like saying the Cathedral of Chartres is so beautiful because it is made of 50,000 stones."

Langlois, by continually rediscovering the cinema of the past and sharing his discoveries, helped create the cinema of the future. And just as he inspired great and abiding love, he also made many enemies. As he achieved much, so he also made mistakes. This is not a work of hagiography, but it would be unfair not to make clear from the start that—"in spite of everything"—he was one of the most admirable and lovable men I have ever met. So although I have no intention of glossing over Langlois's faults, I can only paint an ultimately positive picture. I knew the man for almost twenty years, but since his death I have learned much about him that I did not know. Not all of what I learned is flattering, but there has been nothing to make me revise my fundamental convictions. He was a great man.

A PASSION FOR FILMS

1

The Beginning

H enri Langlois was born on November 12, 1914; the cinema as an art form and an entertainment was by then
almost twenty years old. Most people think of it as beginning
with D. W. Griffith's *Birth of a Nation* in 1915 and consign
everything before that to the status of primitives or forerun-
ners. But Langlois was to show the world that those first two
decades of cinema were not of just historical or antiquarian
interest. By preserving and collecting films, and even more by
his genius as a showman, he made us aware that filmmakers
like Georges Méliès, the Lumière brothers, and Louis Feuil-

lade in France; Edwin Porter and the early D. W. Griffith in America; and Mario Caserini and Giovanni Pastrone in Italy were important directors, and that their films not only were to influence the development of cinema, but were also works of art in themselves.

The first public film show was that of the Lumière brothers in Paris in December 1895. But there are valid claims by other pioneers to have invented the cinema; Edison, for example, has his champions. Langlois, however, maintained that it began with Auguste and Louis Lumière because they were the first to take film out of the box (the Kinetoscope, the peep-show machine for one spectator at a time) and put it up on a screen before an audience. That was what, in a sense, Langlois himself was to do in the cinema archival world— take films out of the cans and put them up on a screen where people could see them. He was to teach us that the Lumière brothers were more than cinematographers, that their films contained many inventive elements of film language: the tracking shot, the "right" angle for showing an action or a place. Georges Méliès's career as a filmmaker was almost at an end in 1914, and he was a forgotten figure by the end of the 1920s. But Langlois taught us that this fairground illusionist, who used film to extend his range of tricks, was a real film-maker who developed the possibilities of storytelling on film. And Louis Feuillade (whose five-part serial Fantômas had broken upon the world a year before Langlois's birth) was shown by Langlois to be much more than a commercial filmmaker: in 1915, with Les Vampires, he made one of the first great films in the history of cinema.

Langlois was no chauvinist; if French cinema had a special place in his heart, it was a place shared with American cinema. America and France, he thought, were the only two countries to have an unbroken line of important films from

The Beginning

the early days until now. (Other countries had their great periods but also had decades when nothing of importance was being made—Germany in the teens, Italy in the twenties, etc.) He was also among the first to champion the Italian films made before World War I. Of course, it was easier being an internationalist in those days because there were few language barriers: the concept of the "foreign" film came into being with the advent of sound and the necessity for dubbing or subtitling. During Langlois's youth, films crossed national lines easily—all they needed was a relatively cheap series of intertitles in the language of the country they were to be shown in.

This was lucky for the young Langlois, for although of French parentage, he was born far from Paris in the Turkish city of Smyrna (now Izmir). Both the place and the time (1914) of his birth were of great significance. For one thing, he was a born internationalist, having spent the first seven years of his life outside France. Because his father, Gustave, left Smyrna in 1916 to fight in World War I and did not return until 1920, Henri was brought up by three women—his mother, his maternal grandmother, and his beloved Greek nurse-governess, Parona.

Smyrna in those days under the Ottoman Empire was an extraordinary place for foreigners. There were opportunities to make a good living, and Gustave Langlois had established himself as a journalist. He created a French press agency there—L'Agence Nationale Française—but he also had his hand in other things: he bought tobacco futures and was involved in many kinds of import-export deals.

Langlois used to boast that he was one-quarter American. His mother, Annie-Louise Braggiotti, was born in Smyrna in

1884 into a family of Italian descent who had emigrated to America before the Civil War. Annie-Louise's mother had been born in Charleston, South Carolina. After the Civil War, the family left the United States because, Langlois thought, they had been on the losing side.

Although Smyrna belonged to Turkey at the time Henri Langlois was born, it had been and still was in many respects a Greek city, and Greek was the language most commonly spoken. It was very much an international city, with many foreign concessions: French, Italian, German, English, American. There still existed what was called a *"régime de ca-pitulation"*; the house in which the Langlois family lived, and even their garden, were considered to be French soil.

Gustave Langlois returned to Smyrna in 1920, and in that same year his second child, Georges, was born. Meanwhile, Henri had already begun going to the cinema. There is no record of what films he saw during his childhood, and, indeed, the war might well have prevented many films from reaching Smyrna. He did remember seeing *The Count of Monte Cristo* and *Jeanne d'Arc*, and these two films confused him. Both were set in France, and his father was then in France. But his mother explained to him that it was not the *same* France. So young Henri decided that there must be three Frances—the one where his father was, the one where *Jeanne d'Arc* was set, and the one in which the Count of Monte Cristo had his adventures. He said that this was an important moment in his life, the first discovery of the relation between space and time, a relation which lies at the heart of narrative filmmaking.

After Germany and its Turkish allies were defeated in 1918, Smyrna was captured and occupied by Greek troops. The 1920 Treaty of Sèvres officially gave Smyrna to the Greeks, but, as Langlois's brother Georges put it, no provision 'was made for them to keep it. And soon, in 1922, the

new regime of Kemal Atatürk invaded this rankling Greek enclave on Turkish soil and retook the city. The earlier violence of the Greeks was answered by the Turks. French, British, and American battleships stood in the harbor, but only to save their compatriots; they did nothing to prevent the massacre of Greeks: three fifths of the city was destroyed.

During the siege the Langlois family were safe in their house; groups of Greeks and Armenians took refuge in the garden. "We were always a generous family," says Georges Langlois, "and we took in as many people as we could."[1] But when incendiary bombings began and there were fires everywhere, Gustave decided it was time to go. They put into one big valise everything of value they could carry: silver plate, gold, jewelry. "Father took the suitcase, mother took me, the baby, in her arms, and Henri, who was nearly eight, put on his best clothes—a sailor suit. We also took our maternal grandmother and Parona, the Greek maid, and set out for the French consulate." Georges Langlois tells the story not from personal memory (he was barely two), but from what his parents and brother told him later on. The streets were full of mobs; there were troops everywhere, and the French consulate was barricaded against the hundreds of Greek refugees trying to get in, with the locked gates guarded by marines. Little Georges fell in the struggle; he wasn't hurt, but when the family finally succeeded in getting in—thanks to the marines holding off the Greeks at bayonet point—they discovered that the suitcase with all the valuables was gone. The father thought the mother had it, and vice versa. It had been left behind in the mob outside, and was never recovered. Fortunately, Gustave had some money with him.

They were put onto a French battleship and after arriving in Marseilles went on to Paris and a new life. Gustave had counted on help from his brothers, all of whom he had sent to France to study and whom he had supported there, but, according to Georges Langlois, they were not as generous as Gustave had expected. The family did receive a small indemnity from the French government, just enough to buy some furniture for a flat they rented on the rue Laferrière in the 9th Arrondissement of Paris. The apartment, Georges remembers, was nice, but the street was not.

So Gustave had to make a fresh start at the age of forty-three. He had been profoundly distressed during the siege of Smyrna by what he thought to be the cowardly nonintervention of the French (as well as the other Allies), and he wrote graphic reports about it for the French press. But these were never published, and he himself was more or less boycotted by the newspaper profession. Disgusted with this dishonesty, Gustave gave up journalism for good and cast about to see what else he could do to support his family. He had always been something of an inventor, and he got a job with the Fonderie Strasbourgeoise, a company that manufactured train equipment. Not only was he their salesman, but he also invented gadgets for them, such as a "purger," an apparatus that got rid of the water that collected in heating pipes which used steam from the train locomotive to heat the coaches. With the royalties from this and other inventions, plus his commissions on sales, the family managed to get along quite well. But his job meant that he was often absent from home.

Even before Henri started collecting films he was already something of a showman. "When I was five and he was twelve," his brother Georges told me, "he would sit me on a little stool, hang up a sheet, put a light bulb behind it, and do all kinds of magic lantern tricks—so I was, with our mother, his first audience."

Their mother (whom Henri often called Gustavette) was by all accounts an exceptional woman. She was cultivated and intelligent, did watercolors, played the piano, and used

The Beginning

to coach Henri in English irregular verbs. Henri taught her to love the cinema, says Georges. He was not so lucky with his father. Langlois's friends say that he and his father did not get on well at all and that Gustave was not sympathetic to Henri's passion for the cinema. Georges demurs, saying that perhaps his father was not as interested as his mother, but there were no serious problems between father and son. The few times Henri spoke to me about his father make me think that Georges is wrong: Henri and Gustave were too different to be very close, and the absence of Gustave during Henri's first seven years hadn't helped.

The French have always tended to take the cinema more seriously than we Americans, and, indeed, by 1914 they had captured ninety percent of the world's film market. (By 1919 this share had dropped to fifteen percent.) During the period in which Henri was growing up in Paris, their enthusiasm for the cinema had reached amazing proportions, thanks in large part to the impact of three American filmmakers: Chaplin, of course, but also Erich von Stroheim and Cecil B. De Mille. They were denied the chance of seeing *Birth of a Nation* (purportedly by the French government itself, which was afraid of the effect it might have during a war in which black Senegalese troops played an important role), so their first inkling of the advances in camera work, narrative technique, and subtlety of acting that the American cinema was making came in De Mille's 1915 film *The Cheat*.

By the time Henri had arrived in Paris, the French had been overwhelmed by a revolutionary German film of 1919, Robert Wiene's *The Cabinet of Dr. Caligari*, which demonstrated that realism was not the only mode in which films could be made. How soon young Henri saw it we don't know, but from the way he talked about it—particularly the tinted prints that were made for its French release—it must have been fairly early. In any case, the climate was there for a film culture that no country was to know again until the sixties. It was the beginning of the film clubs, the high-quality film magazines, and the theories of film propounded by critic and filmmaker Louis Delluc (whose name is still memorialized in France in an annual prize for the best film of the year). It was also the era of the first French avant-garde in the cinema: Delluc, Germaine Dulac (who was later to be of great importance in setting up the Cinémathèque), Jean Epstein (whose sister Marie was to become one of Langlois's most trusted collaborators), Abel Gance, and Marcel L'Herbier, whose works Langlois was to champion through the lean years until they finally achieved their rightful place in film history.

In 1922, as now, Paris was full of cinemas. But in those days, there was less distinction between the commercial film and the art film than there is now: *Caligari* was no small-company low-budget film, and the works of Abel Gance were shown in ordinary neighborhood cinemas. It has been said that Langlois preferred the silent cinema to the sound film, but even if this was not entirely true, he did have a special kind of affection for the films he saw as a child (as do many of us). And he saw many, many films, to the despair of his father.

One film we know he saw was *A Girl in Every Port*; years later he was to write that the screening of it in Paris in 1928 was a double discovery—that of the director, Howard Hawks, and that of the star, Louise Brooks: "To the Paris of 1928, which was rejecting expressionism, *A Girl in Every Port* was a film conceived in the present, achieving an identity of its own by repudiating the past. To look at the film is to see yourself, to see the future." So, for Langlois, even at the age of fifteen, there was no dividing line between Hollywood and the avant-garde film. In this he was not unique, for the French tended to rate the products of Hollywood higher than Americans did.

During the years when Louise Brooks was almost totally forgotten elsewhere, Langlois considered her one of the great figures of the cinema. Miss Brooks, he wrote, was

> . . . the modern artist par excellence. . . . Those who have seen her can never forget her. . . . As soon as she comes on the screen, fiction disappears along with art, and one has the impression of watching a documentary. The camera seems to have caught her by surprise, almost without her knowing it. She is the intelligence of the cinematic process, of all that is photogenic; she embodies all that the cinema rediscovered in the last years of silent film: complete naturalness, and complete simplicity. Her art is so pure that it becomes invisible.[2]

The triumph of the sound film only a year after *A Girl in Every Port* was to prove the determining event in Langlois's career. Not because he rejected sound (as did so many film theoreticians and directors) but because he soon realized that it was to endanger the survival of decades of silent masterpieces. As he was to write,

> In the triumphal years of the art of the silent film, years which saw—after *Birth of a Nation* and *The Cheat*—a succession of masterpieces, it never occurred to anyone to imagine that there could ever be people barbarous enough to destroy these films or to let them disappear. At the end of the twenties all the archives of the major production companies of the world were still intact.[3]

It soon became clear that there *were* people barbarous enough to destroy, for example, four thousand Méliès negatives. Of course, it wasn't pure barbarism. Film is a valuable commodity; it can be melted down for its silver salts, and the cellulose content can be recycled. And with the coming of sound, it seemed to many producers and distributors that no one would ever want to see these old films again. The revolution of the talkies was imposed, as Langlois said, by box-office receipts, against the conservative filmmakers and critics. For the first time in the history of cinema, they began to cherish its past and tried to safeguard it.

But their goodwill came to nothing, and as talking pictures became more and more popular, the efforts in favor of the silent film became more and more sporadic. The attempt to maintain, at least in Paris, one repertory cinema devoted to silent film proved vain. By 1932 the struggle was over. The Salle des Agriculteurs, the last important cinema in Paris where one could see regularly the masterpieces of the silent repertory, changed its programming. Its first sound presentation, Hawks's *Scarface*, was an enormous success, so there was no going back. The reign of the talkies was definitive. Silent films had lost all commercial interest and were doomed to disappear or to end up in fairground shows. "The era of the silent cinema," wrote Langlois,

> ended as it had begun. There were still two forgotten cinemas on the Grands Boulevards which had survived thanks to their low ticket prices and because prostitutes could come in to rest their feet without altogether losing the chance of finding a customer. So it was that one could still see in 1934 in Paris *The General* and *The Navigator*, the great Chaplins, the wonderful Douglas Fairbanks films, the later Griffiths—*Battle of the Sexes*, *Lady of the Pavements*, as well as Pabst's *Joyless Streets*, von Sternberg's *Underworld*, and even Dovzhenko's *Earth* and Pudovkin's *Storm over Asia*. Then, in their turn, these two theaters bought sound equipment so that they could raise their prices. . . .

The Beginning

And only the maids, the children, and the fishermen, for a few *sous*, sitting on the benches of the traveling cinemas of Brittany and the Vendée still wept at the expressive gestures of Lillian Gish.[4]

Traveling cinemas were quite important in Europe—indeed these fairground film exhibitors, who used to set up screens and projectors where there was anyone to look at their films, were later to prove an important source of films for the Cinémathèque. The text by Langlois from which I have been quoting (written in 1956 for the sixtieth anniversary of the cinema) concludes thus:

> However, the "silent art" had created too much enthusiasm, had been the object of too exclusive a cult, had created too many vocations to be forgotten so quickly by a generation of critics. And so were born—almost at the same time, but without any concerted action—the first three cinémathèques devoted to conserving and projecting cinematographic works of art: New York, London, and Paris. This was not by chance. Each of these three cinémathèques was the last creation of that great movement of opinion which, from 1916 to 1930, had arisen in favor of the cinema. The last of the film clubs was liquidated, film criticism was paralyzed, everything had fallen to pieces but, before it disappeared, this movement was able to create the cinémathèques.*

*The important difference between the Cinémathèque Française and the archives in New York (at the Museum of Modern Art) and London (at the British Film Institute) was that the Cinémathèque *began* with the idea of showing films as well as preserving them. The British Film Institute started in 1933; its archives section, inaugurated in 1935, did not, with minor exceptions, show films until after World War II. Nor did the Museum of Modern Art have an intensive program of screenings in the thirties. Even after the war, for some years it usually showed only one film a week, twice daily.

If Langlois failed to mention here the first of the archives to be constituted—the one in Stockholm, begun in 1933—it is probably because it was a rather small and unambitious establishment. Nonetheless, Langlois's point stands: the archive movement did result from the passing of the silent film. If many people think of the Cinémathèque Française as the first of the archives, it is because it was the first to show films, because Langlois was as much a showman as a collector, and because interest in film was especially great in Paris.

2

The Bathtub

The legend that the Cinémathèque began in the Langlois family bathtub is one of the best known of the Langlois stories. And like many legends, it is partly true. Not, however, actually in the bathtub, Georges Langlois told me. "After all," says Georges, "we did take baths from time to time." As in many old French apartments, the bathroom was huge—fifteen feet by twelve, probably because it was installed after the house had been built, so a whole room was used—and there was space for storing films.

Langlois's vocation began when his family bought him a

Pathé-Baby projector (this was a 9.5 mm machine, a kind of ancestor of Super-8). "We weren't rich," he said, "but we ate well, if you see what I mean. So, my aunts in Alexandria said that since the machine I wanted was so expensive, I'd have to wait until the Egyptian pound [their principal source of income] rose to two hundred francs. Pretty soon the Egyptian pound did rise, and I got my projector. And so I passed from being a spectator to a film librarian."

The family was not indifferent to films; young Henri was taken to the cinema every Thursday and Sunday afternoon. But they went only to theaters that belonged to the Pathé chain, so he missed, for example, all the MGM films of the period, which were distributed by Gaumont.

He remembered going to the Cinéma des Batignolles in 1929 and seeing a silent film by Jean Grémillon (probably *Gardiens de Phare*), and there he found a neighborhood audience applauding a dream sequence that featured some extraordinary superimpositions. It is not surprising that he was so affected by a dream sequence, for Langlois discovered surrealism at an early age. The most famous surrealist bookshop—José Corti—was then on the rue Blanche, which happened to be on Henri's way to school, the Lycée Condorcet. This was his first contact with contemporary literature, but he was most impressed by the precursors of surrealism, Rimbaud and Lautréamont; and their works became his bibles. "I still remember," he wrote, "the enthusiasm I felt when I read the Surrealist Manifesto," but he also remembers how disappointed he was when he read André Breton's all too personal and all too unrevolutionary prose fiction *Nadja:* "I couldn't understand how such a Manifesto could lead to a work like that. On the other hand, when I saw *Un Chien Andalou*, I was delirious."[1]

The discovery of surrealism was not a turning point in his

intellectual life; it simply confirmed something that he had already been prepared for since his childhood viewings of the films of Ferdinand Zecca and Émile Cohl—naive pioneer filmmakers who were nevertheless ahead of the whole surrealist movement of the twenties. "I am convinced," he wrote in 1965, "that surrealism preexisted in cinema. Feuillade's *Les Vampires* was already an expression of the twentieth century and of the universal subconscious."[2] And indeed, although Feuillade had been thought of as a mere maker of melodramas about stolen documents, kidnapped heroines, and villains who wanted to rule the world, and as such had been despised by the French avant-garde filmmakers of his time, his films— through his visual genius for the protosurrealistic images— transcended the genre.

As one might expect, school came a rather poor third after the frequent visits to the cinema and to the José Corti bookshop, and in fact, Henri was not a good student—except in the two subjects that really interested him: French and history. So at that time of decision which still arrives for every French boy or girl, the *baccalauréat* examination, informally known as the *bac*, he was not well prepared. In those days— and even now—few Frenchmen went to a university; a *lycée* education was considered sufficient for most careers, but it was all-important that the *bac* be passed. Henri did not pass his. His brother Georges says that Henri did write his French literature dissertation (part one of the *bac*) but got a zero in it. He had, says Georges, dared to compare Molière (the subject of the dissertation) with Charlie Chaplin. So he came home and said to his father that since he got a zero in his *best* subject (French), there was no point in taking cram courses or going back for another year. He was poor in math, chemistry, and physics, so what would be the point? According to Georges, his father gave in. Henri's friend and colleague

A PASSION FOR FILMS

Lotte Eisner, however, says that he never even took the exam, because on the day it was scheduled he went to two double-feature film programs.

Langlois's version, given to me in the seventies, was slightly different. He didn't *want* to pass the *bac* because that would have made him his father's prisoner: he would have been obliged to study law, as his brother was later to do.

In any case, his father felt obliged to find him something to do. He was, his father thought, a very unorganized and messy boy who needed to learn some sense of order. So Gustave sent him to work in a printing shop on the rue Montmartre run by a woman who took in young people to train them in filing and classification. Through her wide circle of friends, she was then often able to place her apprentices with the Social Security Administration.

Another young man working there was Jacques, the twin brother of Georges Franju. Before doing his military service, Georges Franju had been a set decorator for vaudeville theaters from 1929 to 1932. He didn't design sets, he merely executed them. Then, after his military service, he began designing cinema posters. In 1934, he got a letter from Jacques saying that he had met an incredible fellow called Henri Langlois: "He's completely crazy, but mad about movies: you'll like him a lot."

When Franju came back from Brittany with his poster maquettes, he found that his brother had left the lady on the rue Montmartre, so he took his place in the printing shop. Franju discovered that Henri, then twenty years old, was indeed very messy, and, as Franju was by nature very tidy, they decided that in order to hang on to their jobs Langlois would make the messes and Franju would clean them up. "That's how we managed to stay on there for about ten months," Franju told me.

The Bathtub

In those days, Langlois was thin to the point that well-meaning hostesses would try to force food on him or take him aside and tell him he had to build himself up. In one surviving photograph of him in the thirties, he is recognizable only by his enormous eyes—which look even bigger in that thin face. In spite of his reputation for messiness he looks as elegant as Franju, though perhaps Langlois had made an effort on the occasion of the snapshot.

The two young men hit it off immediately. Just as he had played the showman with his little brother, so Henri began to teach Franju about the cinema. Brought up in a small town in Brittany, Franju had never heard of the films that Henri would rave about. Franju's first experience with the avant-garde, for example, was a visit to Studio 28, where he saw a double bill consisting of Buñuel's *Un Chien Andalou* and Jean Epstein's *The Fall of the House of Usher*.

Studio 28, which still exists, was one of the few important art houses. Perched on a steep side street in Montmartre, it was off the beaten path, but people found their way there after the scandal caused by the first screenings of *Un Chien Andalou* and *L'Age d'Or*. Franju was fascinated by these two Buñuel films, partly because Langlois had prepared him to "receive" them. Langlois also told Franju of other places where films of this kind could be seen.

The two men then decided they wanted to found their own *ciné-club*. A film theorist, Jean Mitry, who at that time had his own *ciné-club*, helped them at first: not only did he know a lot about old and new films, classics and "primitives," he was able to give the two men practical information, such as the addresses of film distributors who would rent films to noncommercial clubs. They hesitated for a while but finally took the leap. They hired a tiny screening room on the Champs Élysées, and put on a program called "Le Cinéma Fantastique" (again the surrealist influence). This was the first activity of what later became the Cercle du Cinéma.

It was a long program: Epstein's *The Fall of the House of Usher*, Wiene's *The Cabinet of Dr. Caligari*, and Paul Leni's American film *The Last Warning*. How they got the money to rent the films and the screening room is unclear: Franju thinks it was probably a loan from Langlois's father. Gustave may have suddenly decided that there might be some money in the cinema after all; more likely Mme. Langlois managed to persuade him. In any case, people came, the show was a success, and they had enough money to continue.

But their ambitions went beyond running a film club. Langlois and Franju wanted to create a permanent film library—a *cinémathèque*. This was not a new idea—people had been talking about it ever since 1912, and the very word was coined by the film critic Léon Moussinac in the September 9, 1921, issue of *Cinémagazine*. But in the early days the emphasis was more on film as a record of contemporary history than on film as an art form. By the early thirties, however, the idea of a film library as the equivalent of an art museum was firmly established. Langlois and Franju wanted not just to collect and preserve films, but also to show their collection. A *cinémathèque* would be different from the film clubs in that ideally it would not have to depend so much on "popular" programming for an audience; and of course film clubs did not preserve films, they simply showed what was currently in circulation.

But how to start? They needed money and they needed help. And here it was, oddly, that Langlois's father once again provided the answer. Somehow Gustave had come across a man called Paul-Auguste Harlé, the publisher of the French film trade weekly *La Cinématographie Française*, and introduced Henri to him. Since Harlé not only published a magazine, but also printed it, and had a side line in film-poster printing, Langlois showed him Franju's poster designs and asked what he thought of them. He didn't want to ask him right away for help for a *cinémathèque*, even though Harlé had written in his magazine about the need to preserve old films. Eventually, Langlois explained what he had really come to see him about, and Harlé agreed to help. He gave Langlois and Franju ten thousand francs—a lot of money in those days—to buy prints with. The first purchase was *The Fall of the House of Usher* and the second, *Birth of a Nation*. In 1935 the Cinémathèque Française was established, and the statutes were signed by Langlois and Harlé on September 2, 1936.

Then came the problem of a place to store their films—besides the Langlois bathroom—and again Harlé helped them. He had previously urged them to persuade Alexandre Kamenka, president of Albatross Films, the leading avant-garde producer of the twenties, to deposit his films with the Cinémathèque, and Kamenka agreed; but he wanted to know where they were going to be kept. Fortunately, Franju knew the director Georges Méliès very well; at that time he was living in a home for retired people in Orly, a suburb of Paris. Méliès showed Langlois and Franju a broken-down building in the park attached to the home at Orly. The building belonged to the muncipality, and Harlé paid the town for the building, as well as for fixing it up; the key was given to Méliès, thus making one of the first film directors the first "curator" of the Cinémathèque.

The Kamenka collection (which included René Clair's *The Italian Straw Hat* and *Les Deux Timides*, Jacques Feyder's *Carmen* and *Les Nouveaux Messieurs*, and films by the Russian expatriates) started the ball rolling, and Harlé kept introducing Langlois and Franju to other producers. He and Langlois did not continue to see eye to eye, however, and soon Harlé re-signed his post as president. He was the first—but not the last—benefactor with whom Langlois quarreled. Langlois was, even then, what is called "difficult" (Franju prefers the word "turbulent"), and, although he could be the most ac-complished of diplomats when it suited him, he could also suddenly turn on people for real or imagined slights. In this case the two men remained friends, but at a distance.

Given Langlois's temperament and the lack of money and personnel, the films were not cataloged in the usual sense—all that training in filing and classification at the print shop of the rue Montmartre went for nothing. Langlois had his own methods, which consisted of an excellent memory and a series of schoolboy's notebooks in which he wrote down whatever he felt he had to, but which were not easily decipherable by anyone else.

He made no attempt to examine carefully the condition of the films, nor did he have money for preserving them scientif-ically (if indeed there is any "scientific" way to preserve ni-trate film). Langlois believed firmly that the best way to preserve films was to show them. Films, he would say, are like Persian carpets: they have to be walked on. Projecting films did at least get them aired, so that any gases that had collect-ed in the cans were dissipated. In any case, Langlois always felt that the greatest urgency was to get his hands on the films—they must not be lost or melted down. The second pri-ority was to show them, and that function was served by his other enterprise, the Cercle du Cinéma.

Meanwhile, he and Franju actually made a short film to-gether in 1935. Called Le Métro, it has not been seen by any-one since World War II, and all my requests to Langlois to see it were fobbed off with "Later, later." I asked Franju about the making of the film, and he told me that Langlois refused to

The Bathtub

touch the camera, saying that he was too clumsy and that somehow he would mess up the film if he shot any of it.

Was Langlois a frustrated filmmaker? He has said that he told his father that he wanted no other career than the cinema—but he then added the phrase, "and, by ricochet, the Cinémathèque," which would seem to indicate that he indeed wanted to make films himself. Kenneth Anger, an American independent filmmaker who knew Langlois very well over many years, says that Langlois was a frustrated director: Langlois wrote a lot of Feuillade-like scripts which he showed to Anger, scripts full of paranoid intrigue. Langlois once told me that he gave up all notions of directing when sound came in because he couldn't conceive of directing a film he hadn't written, and he was incapable of writing dialogue.

Franju's evidence concerning Langlois's fear of the camera would not bear this out. There may have been some kind of block, but if there was, he did fight against it. For example, in 1958 there was a project for a film about Marc Chagall; Langlois had thousands of feet of film shot, but he never got around even to making a rough assembly print. His friend Jean Riboud thinks that he lost interest in Chagall's work as that work—to his mind—deteriorated. But there were probably other reasons. Was he afraid of adverse judgment? Was he inhibited by his knowledge of the history of the cinema—did he know too much about the cinema to risk making a film which would probably not measure up to the masterpieces he loved? Or is there a different and psychological explanation? It is true that he rebelled against his father's desire for him to study law and become a respectable member of society. But perhaps the interdiction of the father was only partially surmountable; he was able to collect and show films but not to become a filmmaker.

☐

L anglois had been brought up almost entirely by women, and he was to surround himself throughout his life with women who devoted themselves to him. The first was Lotte Eisner. She was born in Berlin in 1896, and after taking a Ph.D. in archaeology and art history she began writing film criticism in 1927 for the *Film Kurier*, a daily film-and-theater newspaper. She stopped writing for the *Film Kurier* on March 31, 1933, the day the magazine was taken over by the Nazis. Since her sister had married a Frenchman, she decided to leave immediately for Paris. Her brother said: "Why are you leaving now? You're crazy. This whole thing will blow over soon." She only said: "You'll see. I'm leaving now, and I'm taking with me all my books and belongings. When you leave, it will be with an overnight bag." And sure enough, in 1938 Mlle. Eisner heard a knock on her door in Paris, and there was her brother with a small suitcase.

She had read in the *Cinématographie Française* a little piece about two young men who were trying to save silent films. Soon after her arrival in Paris she met Henri Langlois. This was in 1934. "I liked silent films a lot: they had something that the talkies seem to have lost . . . the atmosphere, the mood was different. I arranged a meeting with Langlois and Franju: we were all to turn up at the Café Wepler, place de Clichy, with a copy of the *Cinématographie* under our arms. We got on together immediately, and whenever I had the time (I was making my living by writing for a Czech film magazine), I helped them sort stills, posters, and programs. He already had in mind the future Museum of the Cinema."

Langlois's relationship with Lotte Eisner was platonic. Indeed, he was not to have a serious relationship with a woman until he was over twenty-five. His first sexual experience, he

The Bathtub

once told me, was the classic visit to the brothel, with the classic reaction of disgust and impotence. Later, however, he said, someone introduced him to the equally classic understanding older woman, and things went very well. The first love of his life was for Catherine Hessling. Mlle. Hessling had been a model for the painter Auguste Renoir and later became the wife of Jean Renoir, starring in many of his early films (*Nana*, *La Fille de l'Eau*, and others). By the time Langlois met her she had been separated for some time from Renoir, but it always seemed to me as if Langlois had fallen in love as much with Renoir's vision as with the lady herself. She may have felt this; in any case she had a lover whom she was not prepared to give up for Langlois.

In addition to Lotte Eisner's moral support, Franju told me, the Cinémathèque received valuable assistance between 1936 and 1938 from three influential women. Germaine Dulac, one of the important avant-garde French filmmakers of the 1920s, brought aid from the major film companies: "Mme. Dulac had a great deal of authority; she came from an important family, and she was rich, but adorable, and incredibly devoted." There were two others: Germaine Dulac's friend Yvonne Dornès, who at that time was Mme. Bacheville, *chargée de mission* to Yves Chataigneau, then Secretary General of the State Council. The third woman was Mlle. Suzanne Borel (later Mme. Georges Bidault), who at that time was head of the *Oeuvres Françaises à l'Étranger*, a service dependent on the Ministry of Foreign Affairs, which represented French culture abroad—the press, the radio, the cinema. Through her they had access to the diplomatic pouch, which was of great help to them.

The Cercle du Cinéma and the Cinémathèque had a distinctive policy of collecting and programming. Franju has told us of Langlois's interest in surrealist and experimental films, but Langlois was bent, from the start, on saving and screening all (or almost all) films. Most important, he refused to accept the judgment of film critics and historians about films of the past. Strange as it may seem, before 1936 he had never seen Jean Renoir's first important film, *Nana*. It had a bad reputation in France. But after looking at some stills he decided that it could not possibly be without interest, so he screened *Nana* for himself and immediately saw that it was an important film.

Nana was among the first films saved by the Cinémathèque, along with Renoir's preceding film *La Fille de l'Eau*. Georges Sadoul saw *Nana* at the time and reported that although the technique and the acting in certain scenes were dated, the work remained magnificently powerful. "Its loss would have been irreparable."[3]

One great difference between Langlois's policy and that of the world's other archives is that he did not believe in selection. Langlois even felt obliged later to take to task his great friend Iris Barry, who, when offered all of Buster Keaton's films for the Museum of Modern Art, decided that she would only save "the best." How can I choose, asked Langlois, when a film like Feuillade's *Barrabas* was considered for so long to be of no interest? Obviously, some element of choice was dictated by the Cinémathèque's limited budget. But from the very beginning Langlois assumed that all the work of any director he considered to be of interest was worth saving. In that sense, he was the first of the "auteurists."

Renoir was a director Langlois much admired—although that did not stop Langlois from writing a somewhat critical review* of *The Lower Depths* (*Les Bas-Fonds*) when it came out. The two men became friendly in the late thirties, but

*In *Cinématographe*, March 1936.

they occasionally had their problems. Langlois once told me that when Renoir gave him a lift after a screening of some rushes of *The Rules of the Game* (*La Règle du Jeu*), he remarked how clever Renoir had been to choose an ugly woman (Nora Gregor) to play the aristocratic heroine, since, said Langlois, most of the great aristocrats were ugly. Renoir said nothing, but looked grim; later Langlois found out that Renoir had been in love with Nora Gregor and did not think she was at all ugly.

Another filmmaker whose early work caught Langlois's attention was Marcel L'Herbier. As Georges Sadoul pointed out, "Renoir's then current films might have consoled us for the loss of *Nana*. But this was not the case with L'Herbier: any young man today would find it difficult to believe that he had once produced some remarkable films."[4] One of those great works of the 1920s was *Eldorado*, which along with other L'Herbier films of that period was saved by Langlois. Sadoul went on to rejoice that "all of Delluc is now at the Cinémathèque. We can see once more *Fièvre* and *La Femme de Nulle Part*, as well as Epstein's *Coeur Fidèle*, one of the great moments of cinema. All the Feyders are there, and *L'Image* was bought for 400 francs at the very moment when it was about to fall into ribbons on the travelling cinema circuit. And that film, along with *Gribiche*, *Carmen*, *Visages d'Enfants* and others, will show the path that Feyder took to arrive at *Pension Mimosas* and *Carnival in Flanders*. *Un Chien Andalou* and Buñuel's *L'Age d'Or*, these masterpieces of the avant-garde period, have been conserved by the Cinémathèque, and we will be able to compare them with his forthcoming film, *Land without Bread*. The greater part of René Clair's *oeuvre* has also been found."

As Sadoul also pointed out, the Cinémathèque did not preserve only the French heritage. Thanks to some lucky purchases and exchanges it collected important foreign prints. Griffith's *Intolerance* and *Way Down East*, the films of William S. Hart, Rex Ingram, and Stroheim's *Greed*, along with some of the best Swedish and German films of the silent period (*Sir Arne's Treasure*, *The Phantom Carriage*, *Caligari*, *Nosferatu*, films by Pabst and Dreyer). Nor, he adds, must we forget those "strange pre–World War I works by Émile Cohl and Méliès."

Langlois saved many films, like *L'Image*, in *extremis*: their producers had already directed the labs to destroy some of these precious negatives. A few days later they would have been gone forever, melted down for their celluloid: "The comb you use every morning might well have been made from a fragment of *Broken Blossoms*, *The Cheat*, or *Coeur Fidèle*."[5]

The best and first example of Langlois's pioneering interest in Hollywood cinema is the high regard he accorded the films of Howard Hawks; the result was that in the forties and fifties Paris was the only place where one could see most of Hawks's films. In those days, however, the Cercle du Cinéma's Friday-night screenings did not show films like those, because they could be seen at commercial cinemas. As Jean Rouch, the "inventor" of cinema verité and maker of ethnographical films, remembers, he and his friends would go to see *The Gay Divorcée* at the Lord Byron Cinéma on the Champs Élysées; Studio 28 in Montmartre specialized in the Marx Brothers and W. C. Fields; the Studio Bertrand ran the more "difficult" American films; the Pagode showed films like *The Scoundrel*. The Cercle du Cinéma showed only what it was impossible to see elsewhere.

Rouch remembers discovering the Cercle du Cinéma through a prospectus in a Left Bank art gallery called Les Quatres Chemins, where he had gone to see an exhibition of Dali's drawings for Lautréamont's *Maldoror*. One had to be-

The Bathtub

come a member of the Cercle, but that only cost three francs a year. Admission was eight francs for each screening; for students, six francs. The programs, which were sent out monthly to the members, proclaimed in big letters at the top: *Sans Débats* (no discussions). Langlois, although he usually made a brief presentation of the film, was dead against the didactic *ciné-club* tradition.

Langlois's mother had agreed to make their flat the business address of the Cercle du Cinéma, and she, who had never held a job in her life, worked as cashier at the screenings, while his brother Georges took the tickets. The theater's hundred seats were not the usual cinema kind—they were gilt chairs which were not fixed to the floor. The theater was not always full, but one saw the same people week after week: once he started going, says Rouch, it was so exciting that there was no question of doing anything else on Friday night. The programs were very ambitious. In the month of April 1937, for example, one could see on Friday the 8th a program called "Three Exceptional Films" which included Buñuel's *Un Chien Andalou*, Renoir's *Nana*, and Stroheim's *Queen Kelly*. The following week was titled "Homage to Louis Delluc" and included his *Fièvre*, Germaine Dulac's *La Fête Espagnole*, and Pabst's *Joyless Streets*. The following Friday consisted of two films—one German, one Russian. The heading for the German film was "Anti-Soviet Hitlerian film— *Spartakus Bund*" and for the Russian film, "Anti-Hitlerian Soviet film—Pudovkin's *Deserter*." The final week of that month was devoted to "Humor on the Screen" and was made up of Chaplin's *Shoulder Arms*, René Clair's *Italian Straw Hat*, and Protazanov's *The Miracle of St. Georgion*. But Rouch remembers that the film announced was not always the film shown. One night, perhaps that very last week in April, Langlois announced that the print of *Shoulder Arms* hadn't arrived and instead he would show Dziga Vertov's *Enthusiasm*, a very different kind of film indeed. "But there was no question of anyone protesting: it was like a private party or dinner, where you take what you're given and no one dreams of complaining to the host or hostess about the choice of the menu. Langlois, who was young and so skinny then that he used to use copper electric wire to hold up his pants, was very diffident when he made his presentations, shuffling from one foot to the other, always slightly embarrassed to speak in public."

Rouch continued to frequent the Cercle until the war began, but he never met Langlois in those days. Nor did he know the other members of the "Club"—but they all seemed to know each other, and they were the same people he would see at the Café de Flore. Was James Joyce, as the story goes, a frequent attender? Rouch doesn't know, and no one else seems to remember. André Breton, on the other hand, like some of the other Surrealists, he did recognize. The Prévert brothers, Jacques and Pierre, used to come, and Robert Flaherty put in an appearance. And the intellectual elite came, too—the same people who would later go to the Salle Pleyel to hear Louis Armstrong, or who belonged to Hughes Panassié's Hot Club de France.

3

The Born Internationalist

B y 1938 the fortunes of the Langlois family, thanks to Gustave's royalties on his inventions, had sufficiently improved for them to move from the flat on the rue Laferrière to the more fashionable rue Troyon, near the Champs Élysées and the Arc de Triomphe.

That same year, the Fédération Internationale des Archives du Film (FIAF) was founded. Again, women played an important part. The idea of FIAF, says Franju, came from Germaine Dulac, who put forth the sensible suggestion that the Cinémathèque needed relations with the two similar organizations that had been formed abroad, so that each could benefit from the other collections. FIAF was founded by Langlois and Franju, and two extraordinary women: Olwen Vaughan and Iris Barry.

"In 1938," said Franju, "we spoke about this project to Olwen Vaughan, then Secretary of the British Film Institute. We had met her through Alberto Cavalcanti, the Brazilian filmmaker who at that time was working in Britain with the Grierson/British documentary movement. She was an incredible, unbelievable, but marvelous woman." She was indeed, as I can testify, for I knew her from the time Langlois introduced me to her in 1960 until her death in 1973. Psychologically, she was not unlike Langlois: as Dilys Powell wrote in the *Sunday Times* obituary: "She lived in a state of organized confusion which always came out right: the film hadn't arrived, but somehow she would rescue it; the cook had absconded, but somehow dinner would be beautifully served."

Born in 1905, Olwen was the daughter of a Unitarian minister, the Reverend Hemming Vaughan, who had started the Merseyside Film Society; he believed that cinema was a good thing for mankind. During her reign at the British Film Institute, the archive was founded (in June 1935) and it was she who hired Ernest Lindgren to run it. But she was not really made for administrative duties, and she often quarreled with the director of the BFI, Oliver Bell, as well as with Lindgren. When, in the course of a court case involving the British Film Institute, the judge asked whether she didn't think it unusual to keep the institute's books, as she did, in pencil, she grandly replied, "Well, since they keep changing their minds so often, I use a pencil because it's easier to erase."

Langlois, Franju, and Olwen Vaughan became good friends when they first met in 1938 and began to discuss the formation of FIAF. At that time there was an exhibition of Ameri-

The Born Internationalist

can paintings from the Museum of Modern Art in New York at the Jeu de Paume Museum in Paris. This brought to Paris the curator of the film library of the Museum of Modern Art, Iris Barry, and her husband, John Abbott, the museum's financial director. Almost immediately, Iris Barry and Langlois became friendly, and it was decided that FIAF would have three founder-members: the Cinémathèque Française, the Museum of Modern Art Film Library (represented by Barry), and the British Film Institute (represented by Vaughan). Barry became such an important person in Langlois's life and in that of FIAF that her story must be told here.

Iris Barry, like Olwen Vaughan, was British. Born in Birmingham, England, in 1895, educated there and at the Ursuline Convent in Verviers, Belgium, she first became an assistant librarian of the School of Oriental Studies at the University of London. Her interest in film began when she saw the first French version of *Les Misérables*, probably in 1913. By 1924 she had become the film critic for *The Spectator* magazine; it was the distinguished economist John Strachey (whose father was editor of the magazine) who had the idea that film was important enough to merit a serious film critic. Her first husband was Alan Porter, literary editor of *The Spectator*. Because of her reviews, she was asked by Michael Balcon, Sidney Bernstein, Ivor Montagu, and Adrian Brunel to become a cofounder of the London Film Society. This was the first such organization in Britain, and it boasted such distinguished guarantors as H. G. Wells, G. B. Shaw, J. B. S. Haldane, and Roger Fry.

After initial opposition from the trade and the press, the London Film Society, established on October 25, 1925, became a smashing success. As Ivor Montagu put it, "Half the snobs in London, intellectual and social, were at the opening. Iris, who had flung herself into the thick of the battle, more

than held her own in a tall black superpoke hat with a wide
brim and wide scarlet ribbon, like a witch."[1]

Barry's success on *The Spectator* led to her being offered a
job on the *Daily Mail*, an important London newspaper,
which paid more money and had more influence—and she
took it. Iris Barry was also interested in literature; she wrote
poetry, and it was published. She was even granted an interview by Ezra Pound, who was interested enough in the poems
to want to meet the poet. She soon got to know T. S. Eliot,
Herbert Read, W. B. Yeats, Maud Gonne, and—most important in some ways—Wyndham Lewis. It is said that they became lovers for a time. Indeed, there is a story that when
Lewis passed through New York in the late thirties, he
phoned Barry to invite her to lunch. Lunch went fairly
smoothly, so Lewis thought, but Barry was fuming all the
while. After coffee, she exploded, "You haven't even asked
me about our children!" To which Lewis is supposed to have
replied, "Oh, was there more than one?"

The first big change in her life came in 1930. Her marriage
with Porter had broken up; she had had a run-in with the editor of the *Daily Mail* and was fired. It was time to start again,
so she went to America. After a period of translating, ghost-
writing, and book reviewing, she landed a job with the newly
founded Museum of Modern Art. She was hired to help bring
out a series of monographs on modern artists. At that time
there was no film department, although the first director of
the museum, Alfred H. Barr, Jr., had proposed in a report
written in 1929 for the founding trustees that the museum
should include commercial and industrial art, theater design,
film, and photography, alongside the museum's collection of
sculpture and painting. The trustees, however, rejected most
of these proposals, reasoning, Margareta Akermark (Barry's
assistant and later associate director of the film department)

tells us, that the museum would be lucky to weather its first years even if it limited itself to painting and sculpture. So the "1929 Plan" went underground.

In 1932 Alfred H. Barr published the following statement in a museum pamphlet called *The Public as Artist*: "That part of the American public which should appreciate good films and support them has never had a chance to crystallize. People who are well acquainted with modern painting or literature or the theatre are amazingly ignorant of modern film. The work and even the names of such masters as Gance, Stiller, Clair, Dupont, Pudovkin, Feyder, Chaplin (as director), Eisenstein and other great directors are, one can hazard, practically unknown to the Museum's Board of Trustees, most of whom are very interested and very well informed in other modern arts. . . . It may well be said without exaggeration that the only great art peculiar to the 20th century is practically unknown to the American public most capable of appreciating it."

Encouraged by Alfred Barr, Iris Barry set about the task of finding support and money for the future film library of the museum. She had to convince the money men and the film trade, and she succeeded in doing both. Architect Philip Johnson helped her, and John Hay Whitney put up money for a preliminary study of what a film collection should be. Meanwhile, she had remarried, and with her second husband, John Abbott, arranged a large grant from the Rockefeller Foundation; then, with Whitney's help, they both went to Hollywood to explore the problems.

There she pulled off one of her most brilliant coups: she got Mary Pickford and Douglas Fairbanks to lend her their mansion, Pickfair, considered to be the most exclusive home in Hollywood, for a screening of *All Quiet on the Western Front*, and persuaded Miss Pickford to invite all the right people. By this time one of the leading actors in the film, Louis Wolheim, was dead, and the effect of seeing him on the screen suddenly made all of Hollywood realize that they were mortal, but that they might achieve immortality if their films were preserved.

Iris Barry was a clever woman and a persuasive one. Lillian Gish has told us that it was D. W. Griffith's trust in Iris that saved the Griffith collection from destruction. In 1935 the film library was set up, and she became its first curator. And in that capacity she came to Paris in 1938, where she met Langlois and Olwen Vaughan, and the three of them set about founding FIAF.

But there was a fourth person involved as well, a German. I'll let Franju, the only surviving witness, tell the story in his own words:

"We published our intentions of founding FIAF, and suddenly there arrived in Paris at the Hôtel Crillon, where we were meeting, a *bonhomme* called Frank Hensel; he had been sent by the German Reichsfilmarchiv. So we agreed that there would be four founder-members. Langlois and I decided that the seat of FIAF should be in Paris. Langlois was supported by his family, whereas my parents were too poor to send me any money, so we agreed that, since it would be easier to find money in France for an *international* organization, I would be the administrative secretary of FIAF—a paying job—and he would remain the unpaid secretary-general of the Cinémathèque. And so I was elected to FIAF.

"The statutes of FIAF were presented by Yvonne Dornès to Yves Chataigneau, who got our project passed in spite of opposition from the state. And all this was thanks to Yvonne Dornès; at the same time she secured an office on the sixth floor of the Palais Royal. It was the locale of the Office of Intellectual Cooperation, which was the equivalent—under the League of Nations—of what UNESCO was to become under the United Nations.

"From 1938 to 1944 FIAF continued to have its offices there. But from the moment I was physically separated from Langlois, we started to have problems. The first congress of FIAF was held in New York in 1939. I was supposed to go, along with Langlois, Olwen Vaughan, and Frank Hensel, but the stomach ulcer I had suffered from since the age of ten began to perforate, and my doctor wouldn't let me go."

Arthur Knight, who was working at the Museum of Modern Art in those days, remembers vividly going to meet Langlois at the pier. Skinny as a rail, Langlois erupted into New York, says Knight, with tremendous enthusiasm. Although Franju was absent from that meeting, he was confirmed as executive secretary of FIAF; Olwen Vaughan was named treasurer; Langlois, secretary; John Abbott, chairman. And the first president was none other than Frank Hensel. *

It may seem odd—it certainly did to me—that such politically "progressive" people as Langlois, Vaughan, Iris Barry, and especially Franju himself would accept so lightly a German as president, and even the presence of the Reichsfilmarchiv, as late as 1938 when surely, I said to Franju, all right-thinking people were, if not anti-German, at least anti-German government, anti-Nazi.

"Oh," said Franju, "that was no problem in 1938. You know, in those days, it was the Left that was pro-German in France. Those who were most virulently anti-German were

* The twentieth anniversary brochure published by FIAF states that in 1938 John Abbott was elected president, Frank Hensel, vice-president, Langlois, secretary-general, and Olwen Vaughan, treasurer. For 1939, however, it lists Abbott as chairman, Hensel as president, and Langlois and Vaughan as secretary-general and treasurer respectively.

on the right! The Popular Front was all for peace. Hitler was seen wearing a white tuxedo—and people said, 'That's a good sign, he's going to calm down and leave us in peace.' It was right-wing people like François Poncet who said, 'Yes, the Left talks of peace, nothing but peace, while the sky is red with the threat of the Germans.' During the Popular Front, we voted against a war or defense budget. Later I realized that we had been stupid. The Right is hateful, but it was they who were correct and we who were wrong. They saw clearly. The second FIAF Congress, to be held in Berlin in 1940, never took place."

Franju's views can be corroborated by many: even Simone de Beauvoir and Jean-Paul Sartre, pedaling their way across France on bicycles, refused to believe there was any real threat from the other side of the Rhine. Wishful thinking? Intellectual blindness? Pacifist panaceas? It's hard to say now; there are great gaps in our knowledge about the way people thought and behaved during that period.

N ot content with founding FIAF, Langlois was responsible for creating and stimulating many new film archives in this prewar period. Some have cynically maintained that his help and encouragement were a bid for power, an attempt to gain future allies in FIAF. There may have been something to this, but I believe that it was more because Langlois realized that the Cinémathèque Française could not do the job of preserving films alone. Of course, after having helped foreign archives to get going, he expected something in return: prints of films he didn't possess; but I think that such was his enthusiasm for displaying his treasures that he probably gave more than he got.

The first example of Langlois's generosity and enthusiasm was with the Cineteca Italiana (in Milan, and not to be con-

The Born Internationalist

fused with the Cineteca Nazionale, in Rome). The Cineteca Italiana (CI) began as a private film club, founded in 1936 by a young man named Mario Ferrari. He began as a loner, but soon realized the task was too great for one man, and he entered into contact with a group of students who were as *cinéphile* as he was. Among these young men were Luigi Comencini, Alberto Lattuada, Luciano Emmer, and Renato Castellani, all of whom were to become noted directors. They were linked not only by their love of old films but by their antifascism.

Gianni Comencini (brother of Luigi and present director of the CI) tells us that in 1937, soon after the formation of the Cineteca Mario Ferrari, as it was then called, his brother and Lattuada went to Paris, where they became friendly with Langlois. Because of their political views, the first exchanges of films between the two organizations were clandestine: Langlois and others carried the prints back and forth between Paris and Milan hidden in suitcases in third-class carriages. What films did Langlois bring with him to Milan? The most memorable, says Comencini, were Vigo's *L'Atalante* and works by René Clair, Eisenstein, Pudovkin, and Carné.[2]

In those days, Langlois's eccentric eating habits were still not having any effect on his weight. In Milan, Comencini recalls, Henri discovered a particularly good ice-cream shop, and one evening he devoured a dozen portions. That night, at the Comencini house, he began to writhe in agony. Mama Comencini (who seemed to have played as important a role in the CI as Mme. Langlois did in the CF) had an inspiration. Langlois was placed on his back on the kitchen table, and Signora Comencini began to *iron* his stomach. Her theory was that the heat of the iron would thaw out the ice cream. Whatever the scientific merits of her scheme, it worked: the pains stopped.

It has been said, and with some reason, I think, that the

films Langlois brought from Paris were to have a tremendous effect on postwar Italian filmmaking. There were other links, of course: Luchino Visconti had worked as costume designer on Renoir's *Partie de Campagne*; Michelangelo Antonioni was to be assistant on Marcel Carné's *Les Visiteurs du Soir* (*The Devil's Envoys*). But the screenings of Renoir and Carné in the late thirties—in the middle of Italy's "white telephone" school of filmmaking—appear to have influenced Comencini, Lattuada, Emmer, and Castellani.

It was not entirely a one-way street. I think it is safe to assume that Langlois began to become interested in the Italian cinema of the pre–World War I period during those years when he was going back and forth between Paris and Milan.

For most historians, the pre–World War I Italian cinema consisted of just one film: Giovanni Pastrone's *Cabiria*, particularly because it was seen by D. W. Griffith and had an influence on *Intolerance*, but also because it was the first of the superproductions and a great hit all over the world. But Langlois found that there was more to the Italian cinema of the teens. He discovered the cinema of the divas—those incredible Italian superstars like Lyda Borelli, Pina Menichelli, and Francesca Bertini (the last seen as the grandmother in Bernardo Bertolucci's *1900*). There is no denying that on a realistic level these films are grotesque—"camp" before its time— yet they did have a certain romantic folly which, now that we have begun to appreciate again the virtues of melodrama, remains vastly appealing. The titles of these films tell their own stories: *My Love Will Not Die, Royal Tigress, Satanic Rhapsody*. And although it is impossible not to giggle from time to time on seeing, say, *Tigre Reale*, there is nonetheless a sense of grandeur: deranged, if you like, but grandeur just the same.

Oddly enough, *Tigre Reale* was an adaptation of a novel by the "naturalist" writer Giovanni Verga (another of his works

was to supply Visconti with the material for *La Terra Trema*),
and the film was directed by Pastrone, the same man who had
made the very different *Cabiria*. *Rapsodia Satanica* (1914)
starred Lyda Borelli; directed by Nino Oxilia, it tells the ex-
travagant story of a woman who sells her soul to the devil to
regain her youth, only to discover that her heart has remained
old and cold.

At the same time Langlois discovered another side to Italian filmmaking: the protosurrealist and the futurist. One of
these discoveries was a 1913 film by Marcel Fabre, a Frenchman who worked in Italy: the film was *Saturnino Farandolo*. It
is mentioned in none of the film histories (on this side of the
Alps at least; it is not even in Sadoul's multivolume history),
and it gives us a different picture of the Italian cinema of the
period. Its free-floating fantasy, the inventiveness of its sci-
ence fiction make it both entertaining and occasionally quite
beautiful. Thanks to the Cinémathèque and the Cineteca Italiana it was shown at the New York Film Festival's "Spring
Festival" in 1970 on a double bill with Tod Browning's *The
Unknown*, and the sparse audience was captivated by its
blend of naiveté and sophistication. It belongs to a school
qualified by another Italian director of the period,
A. G. Bragaglia, as *pernacchio*. This is the equivalent of
"Bronx cheer," but the phrase has other meanings: liberation
through the absurd, the poetry of the spontaneously incon-
gruous, a purely instinctive and subversive irrationality.

Bragaglia, another of Langlois's discoveries of those years,
was a Futurist, and he and his brother worked out a technique
called *fotodinamismo* which was a kind of recording of movement more complex than anything Marey or Muybridge had
been able to achieve. He also directed two films, *Il Perfido Incanto* and *Thaïs*. Or it appears that he did, because Langlois
discovered that the film he so loved and remembered as *Il Per-*

fido Incanto was actually called *Thaïs*. Did *Il Perfido Incanto* ever exist, or was it an alternative title? Mystery.*

Films like *Thaïs* and *Saturnino Farandolo* give us quite a different picture of Italian cinema of the period, which has usually been thought of solely in terms of *Cabiria*, with a passing mention of the lost neorealist film called, fittingly, *Sperduti nel Buio* (*Lost in the Dark*), the still extant *Assunta Spina*, and *Cenere*, with Eleonora Duse's luminous performance.

What Langlois did for Milan he also accomplished in Brussels. There, André Thirifays had been running a film club since 1930. When he read in a French trade paper about the Cinémathèque, he went to Paris in 1937 to meet Langlois. Langlois was helpful and soon came to Brussels to present a program of films by Feuillade as a benefit for the founding of Thirifays's new Cinémathèque de Belgique.

Meanwhile, the war was getting closer, and Mario Ferrari died suddenly in Milan at the age of twenty-three. The others decided to continue his work, and in 1940 they participated in the Triennale, an exposition of modern art and architecture. The Cinémathèque Française contributed heavily to it—indeed, as we will see, Langlois's attempts to find drawings and maquettes by the great Russian-born French set designer Lazare Meerson first brought him into contact with Mary Meerson, who was to become his life's companion. But he also brought, says Comencini, *La Grande Illusion* by Renoir, a film that was forbidden by Italian censorship at that time. The film had such a tremendous effect on the audience that they all stood up when the French prisoners sang "La Marseillaise." There were spies in the audience, however, some of whom whistled while others went to call the police. The police came so quickly that Luigi Comencini and Lat-

*The Garzanti encyclopedia *Lo Spettacolo* (1976) lists both films.

tuada had to hide in the projection box and from there escape over the rooftops.

That was the end of the Cineteca Mario Ferrari. The war began; the screenings stopped.

The most important person in Langlois's adult life was Mary Meerson, and their relationship is inseparable from the history of the Cinémathèque Française.

Lotte Eisner met Mary before Langlois did. The year was 1939, the place London. "I was having lunch in the Savoy Hotel with Cavalcanti, and suddenly he said, 'Lotte, turn around, and you'll see the beautiful widow of Lazare Meerson.' " Lazare Meerson is generally considered to be one of the greatest designers in the history of cinema, and his sets for the films of René Clair and Jacques Feyder (*Carnival in Flanders*, in particular) were indeed magnificent. He was born in 1897 in Russian Finland, and first began to work in the mid-1920s in Berlin. He came to Paris shortly afterward, and his surviving brother Harry remembers that he met Mary in 1928. He quickly broke into French films and worked closely with René Clair, who depended on Meerson for all the visual aspects of the films they did together. He was a handsome man and a hard worker—he often slept all night in the film studios—but he was also, like Langlois, a very "turbulent" man. Although his sense of humor was dry, and he hardly ever laughed, he was much loved and respected by those who knew and worked with him.

When he met Mary Meerson, she was, if not the Queen of Montparnasse (that title belonged to the famous model Kiki), then at least its Princess. She was an extremely handsome woman, and had modeled for many painters, including de Chirico, Kokoschka (who did a series of portraits of her), and

Kiesling. Who she was and where she came from are still unknown, for if ever there was someone who has surrounded
herself with mystery it is Mary Meerson. No one knows exactly where or when she was born. Lotte Eisner thinks that Mary
is a few years younger than herself, so that would place her
birth date around the turn of the century. That she came
from eastern Europe is also certain, but Langlois and Meerson's brother Harry both said she was born in Bulgaria. She
herself told an interviewer that she was born in Karelia, the
part of Czarist Russia that bordered on Finland (where Lazare
Meerson was born: unconscious identification?). Her maiden
name was Popov, and she certainly speaks Russian fluently
(according to Russians to whom I have spoken), but she also
speaks excellent German, French, English, and Italian. She is
even capable of a few words of Yiddish—which Harry Meerson says she learned from Lazare. Others say that Mary herself
is Jewish.

She and Lazare first lived together in the Hôtel St. Sulpice,
and later moved to an apartment on the rue Gazan facing the
Parc Montsouris. Meerson designed the flat himself, and it
was very much like one of his sets: eggshell lacquer rubbed
with pumice stone to get those off-white tones which gave the
high-key effect of the "white" sets he did for René Clair. She
and Meerson often fought like two cats. He was capable of
throwing the telephone out of the window if he was annoyed,
and she was capable of equally violent behavior. Meerson's
assistant in those days was Alexandre Trauner, soon to become a famous designer himself (*Children of Paradise*), who remembers an evening when he was invited to dinner by the
couple. Mary herself did not arrive until 11 p.m. She berated
them for waiting for her, and stomped upstairs to the loggia
floor. Suddenly Trauner noticed that all the knives had disappeared from the table: the white-gloved Mongolian butler had
silently removed them—just in case.

The Born Internationalist

In 1937 Meerson was called to London by Alexander Korda, and there he did the sets for such films as *Fire Over England*, *As You Like It*, *Knight Without Armour*, *Break the News*, *South Riding*, and *The Citadel*. During the making of King Vidor's *The Citadel* he fell ill. According to Trauner, he had never been a healthy man—afflicted mostly with intestinal disorders—and when he got sick, Korda wanted to send him to a clinic in Switzerland, but it was too late: he succumbed to meningitis in 1938 at the age of forty. Mary had of course accompanied him to London, and she was with him when he died.

Mary stayed on in London for a while after Lazare's funeral, and that is how she happened to be having lunch at the Savoy with Robert Flaherty when Lotte was there with Cavalcanti. According to Lotte, she was as elegant and as beautiful as Marlene Dietrich, and fortunately for those who knew her only later, there does exist a photograph to prove this assertion. After lunch, they all had coffee together.

Lotte did not see Mary again for several years. According to her, Langlois was subsequently introduced to Mary Meerson by Catherine Hessling in Paris in 1941. This does not concur with Mme. Meerson's recollection, which is probably more accurate, since Lotte Eisner was out of Paris after 1940. Mme. Meerson says it was Jean Renoir himself who introduced them. Of course, this could be a "screen memory," since Mme. Meerson either was or soon became aware that Langlois had been attracted to Mlle. Hessling and may prefer to believe that her meeting with Langlois did not come about through a "rival." In any case, this is her version of the momentous meeting:

"I came back from London after Meerson's death, and Jean Renoir came to meet me at the station, accompanied by Alberto Cavalcanti. They took me to the restaurant in the Musée de l'Homme, where we met Bob Flaherty and his daughter

Monica. Renoir told me about a crazy young man that I really ought to meet. Then there was a party at Renoir's, with Catherine Hessling and Cavalcanti, and there was this young man, thin, thin, with very big, prominent eyes. We were introduced, but somehow he got the idea that I was Flaherty's niece! When he found out who I really was, he said, 'You're the one I've been looking for—I need you. I'm trying to arrange an exhibition of Meerson's drawings and maquettes for the Triennale of Milan.' That was an art exhibition, you understand, that covered all forms of fine and applied art and decoration.

"So I said to him, 'Well, come visit me at my flat, rue Gazan.' So he came, along with Luigi Comencini of the Milan *cinémathèque* and Comencini's mother. Comencini brought a letter from Giorgio de Chirico, who was one of the sponsors of the Triennale. I already knew de Chirico; I had posed for him. So of course I gave them what they wanted. By the way, everything I lent to Milan I only got back years later, after the war was over.

"Then came the 'phony war,' and Henri was mobilized for a few months. When he came out of the army in 1940, he came to live with me and my sister Hélène in the rue Gazan. And that's how it all began."

Since the late forties, Mary Meerson has not allowed herself to be photographed, and in spite of increasing shortsightedness, she consistently refuses to wear glasses. Mary Meerson is one of the most (literally) charming persons I have ever met; she can also be one of the most maddening. She can do almost anything, but she must do it her own way, and that way is hardly ever simple. There are those who claim that Mary Meerson was a great handicap to Langlois; on the other hand, she did things for the Cinémathèque that he could never have done. I once heard her talking on the phone to

The Born Internationalist

Jeanne Moreau, then at the height of her fame. "Darling," said Mary, "there is this wonderful dedicated young man in Grenoble who wants to put on a retrospective show of your films, and he would be so glad if you could come to introduce them." I fully expected Mlle. Moreau to tell Mary that it was a ridiculous notion, or at least to explain politely that she had other things to do than to make a six-hour train trip to Grenoble. I could hear only Mary's half of the conversation, but after five minutes Jeanne Moreau had agreed to go.

Mary was adored by Renoir and Rossellini; she had friends in every realm of the arts everywhere. Without her, Langlois told me, the Cinémathèque would never have succeeded in getting its quarters in the Palais de Chaillot in the sixties. Through the telephone she knew everything going on all over the world. She was possessive, she was jealous, and there were people who wondered how Langlois could stand living with her, so much did they quarrel. And yet when he was away from Paris, Henri could not let a day go by without phoning Mary—to check in, as it were, to comfort her, and even more to be comforted. They both had wicked tempers (those who believe in astrology like to point out that they were both double Scorpios). And it was a toss-up as to which was the more paranoid, which the more self-willed. I once dared ask Langlois how it was that he, who had been so extremely thin in the thirties and forties, had become so much heavier later, and he said, "After the war Mary began to put on weight, and so I decided to do the same—to keep her company."

If Mary Meerson could be persuaded to write the story of her life, it would make fascinating reading—but she won't. Nor will she let anyone else; nor will she even *tell* the whole story. Occasionally bits will come out; after seeing the Soviet film *The Last Night*, Mary said to me that it was the one film that really gave an accurate picture of life during the Revolution. "You would go out to a party," she said, "and then you couldn't get home, because the battle lines between Reds and Whites had shifted within the city." But when I asked her, "Where was that, Mary, and when?" she immediately changed the subject.

In her own words, "Mary Meerson does not exist. I am Scheherazade."

4

The German Occupation

The war, the debacle, and the Occupation are periods of French history about which it is still difficult to obtain exact information. With every year, new stories are told that had remained secret. As we saw from Marcel Ophüls's *The Sorrow and the Pity*, many facts and events had been hushed up. And there are different versions of Langlois's activity during this period.

Some things, however, are certain—for example, that Langlois saved a great many films from being seized or destroyed by the German occupying army. Pierre Braunberger told me that if it had not been for Langlois, Jean Renoir's *Partie de Campagne* (which Braunberger had produced) would not have survived; the work print had burned, but Langlois managed to save the negative and at the end of the war gave it back to him. "There were others," says Braunberger, "who 'saved' films, but they were gangsters: at the end of the war they *sold* these 'saved' prints back to me at enormous prices. But not Langlois. He saved and gave back all those films belonging to me and other Jewish producers."

Langlois also helped to save hundreds of American prints. S. Frederick Gronich, director of the European office of the Motion Picture Association of America (MPAA), says, "I have had confirmation of this since, from the German side." It was all done in the usual Langlois manner: "After the war," says Gronich, "one or two of the managers of our companies in France made the rounds with him to pick up their films where they had been stored. There were no pieces of paper exchanged, no records; he just handed them back. He could have kept them, as some archives did, because there were no records. When the war was over, and our offices opened up, we had no prints to show. We couldn't get new films in that quickly, but with the prints Langlois had saved, the film companies were able to get back in business. You know, there was no grandstanding, no big gestures—the films were theirs, and Langlois just gave them back."

These services stood Langlois in good stead with the American companies over the years; but there was an immediate benefit as well: when he started the Cercle du Cinéma again in 1944, he began with a stunning program of films, one from each of the major companies—MGM, UA, RKO, Fox, Warners, Universal, and Columbia—in recognition of the services rendered by the Cinémathèque. These included *Modern Times* (the French-titled print of which Langlois had preserved), *Gone With the Wind, Goin' to Town, Each Dawn I Die, Abe Lincoln in Illinois, Our Town,* and *Young Mr. Lincoln.* How did he do it? This is where the versions are somewhat conflicting. The legend had it that he simply gave films to friends with backyards, or houses in the country, and told them to bury the cans. This was true in some cases, but the story is more complex. When the war broke out in 1939, Langlois was mobilized but was deferred like many others during the "phony war," because there weren't enough guns to go around. He didn't enter the army until 1940, and he was made a telegraph operator. According to his brother he quickly became expert in sending and receiving Morse code. Langlois was sent to a post somewhere on the eastern front, and when the Armistice was signed in June 1940, he, like so many others, simply made his way home.

Once back in occupied Paris Langlois began his safeguarding operations by dispatching some films from the collection to a friend who owned the Château de Beduer, near Figeac in southwest France. Then FIAF was invoked as a means of saving other films. Again, we turn to Franju as a surviving witness of those days. "Although Langlois hid a lot of films, the greater part that he saved were in the Palais de Chaillot, which had been requisitioned for FIAF, and were therefore in my keeping. When the Germans came, there were about three hundred films; when they left, there were three thousand. *Voila!*"

Where did those 2,700 additional films come from? Without taking any credit from Langlois (or from Franju), the truth is that they were able to save so many prints thanks to a German. And not only a German, but Frank Hensel—army officer, Nazi, president of FIAF.

Franju says: "Langlois had collected some, and I cornered some of them, too. There were films that had been seized by the Germans that I had counterseized, thanks to Frank Hensel. When Hensel arrived in Paris, films were all over the place—they had to be gathered together somehow, somewhere, Langlois said. So we got Hensel to requisition the cellars of the Palais de Chaillot."

The Palais de Chaillot figures prominently in the story of the Cinémathèque, so a few words of explanation are necessary for those who don't know Paris. Situated on a hill on the Right Bank, opposite the Eiffel Tower, it was first a country house built for Catherine de Médicis in the second half of the sixteenth century. At that time the area was entirely rural, far from the center of Paris. (Readers of *Manon Lescaut* might remember that this was Manon's first overnight stop on her trip from Paris to Rouen). It then became a convent until Napoleon I decided it made a suitably commanding site for a palace for his son, the so-called King of Rome. Stupendous plans were drawn up, the convent razed, the top of the hill leveled, and the slope evened out. But the builders never got much further than the subbasements. In 1858, a square called the place du Trocadéro was laid out, and twenty years later the site was used to erect a huge Moorish-inspired palace for the 1878 Paris world's fair. In 1937, when Paris had another world's fair, this Trocadéro Palace was torn down and the Palais de Chaillot, an art deco building consisting of two curved wings with a flat open space between them, was built. After the fair ended, the buildings were given over to various museums. (Under that vast flat gap was a huge theater which Jean Vilar was to make famous with his National Popular Theater Company in the fifties, a company which boasted stars of the caliber of Gérard Philipe and Jeanne Moreau.) But in 1939 much of the building remained unoccupied, which is why Hensel was able to requisition the underground vaults.

"I got a key," said Franju, "and, illegally, I gave another to

Langlois. Hensel was not only the director of the Reichs-filmarchiv; he was also a major in the German army. I think he must have been an early Nazi recruit and therefore in a good position. It's also true that his mother was English. He was a very strange fellow. He also had arranged to have an important job with Mitropa, the Ministry of Transportation, because he liked to travel a lot. He got the job at the Reichs-filmarchiv because he was a great film fan . . . and he was also the director of the cinema for the German army.

"So we were always very well informed, and whenever there was a threat of a film being seized by any of the other German authorities, he arranged for a counterseizure, let me know about it, and so I was able to get the film into Chaillot. If it hadn't been for him, I don't know what we would have done. But if he hadn't been such an extraordinary person, I would never have worked with him. It would have been so much easier for me to leave FIAF, to go underground, but I think I did more for France where I was. One thing you must realize: Hensel never knew how many or which films we kept at Chaillot. That was a secret between Langlois and me. He suspected what was going on, but he didn't want to know too much about it. I remember when, ten or fifteen days before the Germans left—before the Liberation of Paris—he came by chance to Chaillot, and he was amazed to find how many films we had there. 'Nice work for Langlois, and for you,' he said, 'but it's better that I didn't know anything about it.' I saw his wife after the war—he liked England, but his wife loved Paris—and she told me that he had had troubles in Germany after the war like the other Nazis, but it didn't last too long. He then went into some kind of business. He had been a circus director at one point in his life, you know—he was really a character. Without him, there would have been no place to store our films.

"Of course, some of them had already been dispersed by Langlois—he had left them here, there, and everywhere, and he was right to do so. I don't know whether you would call Langlois a member of the Resistance, but his resistance consisted of helping a lot of people. Trauner, the set designer, who was Jewish, told me how Langlois managed somehow to get a suitcase with Trauner's most precious belongings from Paris to Vichy, where Trauner could get it."

Detailed information about Langlois during the Occupation is sketchy—and not always reliable. Although public screenings of the Cercle du Cinéma had stopped, Simone Signoret maintains that she saw *Potemkin* during the Occupation in "Mama Langlois's dining room."[1] According to Mary Meerson this could not be true—the *Potemkin* print was 35 mm, and if Mme. Signoret saw it, it was because the Langlois family lived opposite a cinema called the Studio de l'Étoile, where a friendly projectionist would often show films for Langlois and his friends late at night.

Since Langlois's death, some of his detractors—notably Raymond Borde of the Cinémathèque de Toulouse—have tried to make much of the fact that the Cinémathèque, which was to find its first permanent home in a building at 7, avenue de Messine, near the Parc Monceau, was already established there during the Occupation. That building, Borde points out, was the location of the official German film office—the Reichsfilmkammer. The Germans had requisitioned it for various German film services and had built a screening room for the German censors. Now that we know the important role played by Major Hensel in the Cinémathèque's activities during the war, it is easy to see why the Cinémathèque was able to find a home there and also why Langlois and his friends were reluctant to say much about it.

For example, when I asked Langlois's brother Georges if he

remembered the office on the avenue de Messine during the Occupation, he said he had no recollection of it. Five minutes later, when he was showing me some correspondence, we noticed an envelope addressed to Langlois, 7, avenue de Messine! "Odd," said Georges Langlois. "Maybe the Cinémathèque did have offices there. It might have had something to do with Major Hensel." I think that he was sincere; the French have blocked out many things that had to do with the Occupation: even if there was no shame attached to an action, the merest hint of collaboration has been enough to make them disremember. No one seems to mind that the Centre National du Cinéma (still very much in existence as the official government body which gives money for financing films) was also begun (its original name was the Organization Committee for the Cinematographic Industry) during the war—at 7, avenue de Messine. So in fact, the building was used by the Reichsfilmkammer, the Centre National du Cinéma, and—in three rooms on the first floor—the Cinémathèque Française. Oddly enough, according to Franju, it was during the Occupation that the French government offered its first subsidy to the Cinémathèque Française.

Langlois and Franju both took the long view—that their job was to preserve prints, and if they were enabled to do so with the help of the Nazis—or at least one Nazi—then, they felt, they were justified in accepting that help. Just as we recognize that there were some remarkable theater productions put on during the Occupation and some great films made during that period, so I think we have to accept the fact that the French were obliged to use whatever means came to hand to achieve these works. By no stretch of the imagination, for example, can Robert Bresson's first film *Les Anges du Péché* or the stage production of Anouilh's *Antigone* be construed as having given aid and comfort to the enemy. And by the same token, the activities of the Cinémathèque can in no way be construed as "collaborationist," pro-German, or pro-Nazi.

W hile Langlois's principal occupation during the war was the safeguarding of prints, he was also doing his best to safeguard his collaborator and friend, Lotte Eisner, who was Jewish. In 1940, all the Germans in France—Nazis or anti-Nazis—had been sent by the government to a concentration camp in Gurs, near Pau. After four months there, Eisner succeeded in getting out, and made her way to Montpellier. There she found that her French brother-in-law had just gone, but had left behind a little money for her, and she stayed there for a while with friends. Langlois went to visit her from time to time; one day he sent her a letter saying that he had heard the Germans were about to cross the Demarcation Line and invade southern France. "Leave Montpellier immediately," he wrote.

"But suddenly," she recalls, "the Germans were already in Montpellier. I asked my brother-in-law's friends if they knew of any place in a small village nearby where I could stay. 'Yes,' they said, and so I went to this village. I had no money left by now, and I cooked my meals on a Sterno stove—just soup made from bouillon cubes. And then one day, even they were all used up. Suddenly, I met a boy I had known in Berlin. It was at the Montpellier public library, where I went to read André Gide (I *loved* Gide) and he suggested that I could get money from the local rabbi. 'That's funny,' I said, 'because you know my family were very assimilated, and when I went to school I had Protestant religious instruction. I don't know *anything* about Judaism.' But he said, 'Never mind,' and I went with him to see the rabbi. After an hour and a half of waiting, I thought, 'This is ridiculous,' and I walked out.

The German Occupation

Then I met a girl I had known slightly in Paris, and I told her I had come from the rabbi but that I didn't have the courage to see him. 'I don't know the Old Testament, just the New, and that's a little funny to go see a rabbi on.' 'Never mind,' she said, 'I'll take you to a Protestant pastor, and he'll give you money.' So I went to the pastor, told him my story, and he said, 'You're an interesting case!' So I got some money.

"But then one day I was summoned by the police, and I decided it was time to get away from Montpellier for good. Henri said to me, 'Go to Nice—there are no Germans there, just Italians.' 'No,' I said to Henri, 'I want to go to a small town.' And I was glad, because several weeks later the Germans took over Nice and many people were arrested.

" 'Well,' said Henri, 'I have hidden films like *The Great Dictator* and some Soviet films in a castle which belongs to Mme. Jean Voilier, who is half for the Resistance and half for the Germans. Go there as Mademoiselle Escoffier'—my pen name in those days—'and you can see if the films are all right. I had to take them there in a hurry,' said Langlois, 'and I took them in rusty cans, but I would like to know if the prints are still in good condition. Could you make a list of them and stay there for the time being? We can supply you with a letter from the Cinémathèque Française saying that you are compiling lists of German films.'

"I said, 'Well, I'll do that.' It was in a small town near Figeac. Of course, the films were all nitrate, so I couldn't make a fire to keep warm, and I broke all my nails opening those rusty cans, but I made sure the films inside were complete and in good condition. It took me a month to check them all; then I hid the films in the dungeons and covered them with straw. I wrote to my pastor friend in Montpellier asking for work, but all he could find me was a job as a cook in a girls' school. I took the job, but I didn't like cooking very much, and I had to cook for eighty-three people on a wood/coal stove, which was very difficult. After six months I was asked to leave.

"I didn't dare take a train—the railroad stations were always patrolled by the German soldiers, so I went to see an aunt of Georges Sadoul who lived in Figeac and who had rooms to rent. Meanwhile I had given Henri a ring I had from my great-aunt, and he had sold it for me, so I had a little money. But Mme. Guittard said, 'Come live with me for free.'

"Henri came from time to time to see me, and so I stayed with this lady. Then a new problem arose. On my fake identity card, I had made myself a few years younger than I really was, and I discovered that I had made myself so young that I could be drafted to work for the Germans. So I wrote to Henri and asked him to give me a letter on official paper saying that I was working for the Cinémathèque.

"I didn't know then that Henri had friends in the Resistance and that they had stolen letterheads from the Ministry of Culture in Vichy. I don't know if it was actually he who stole them, but in any case I got a letter saying I was an official employee of the Cinémathèque Française. When a German soldier started looking too closely at my identity card, I'd just thrust this letter at him.

"So I was able to stay there until the end of the war. When Henri sent word for me to come to Paris, Mme. Guittard said, 'Don't go yet, the trains aren't running properly,' so Henri came by car to get me and said, 'My dear, your place is at the Cinémathèque Française, and we now have a real home on the avenue de Messine.' They had got it from the Ministry of Information. I loved that building—Henri was to have his first real exhibition there, one devoted to the animated drawings of Émile Reynaud. Oh, yes, I forgot—I went back to Paris with Henri, but first we went to get the films out of the château, and we discovered that they were all safe and sound. The Germans had never even gone near there. Georges Sadoul had alerted the Resistance [the Maquis], and they somehow drew the Germans away from the château.

"Of course, when I got back to Paris, I found that Mary Meerson had entered Henri's life. He had already written me in Figeac that he'd met a beautiful woman and that her name was Mary Meerson. And I thought, 'She's the woman I met in London in 'thirty-nine. Mary and Henri had been living together for four years, and for the next six years she made life very difficult for me. She was jealous, even though Henri and I were only friends. Never anything else. Of course, Mary had had trouble herself with Henri's mother—'that Foreigner,' she would call Mary. Maybe Mary took out on me some of what she had suffered from Mme. Langlois. Well, all that's forgotten now, and Mary and I are good friends."

5

Children of the Cinémathèque

L anglois was never the president of the Cinémathèque—
always secretary-general. In the early days there was not
much need for a president. But during the war, just after the
release of Jean Grémillon's most successful film, *Le Ciel Est à
Vous* (*The Woman Who Dared*), Langlois asked Grémillon to
be the president, even though the Cinémathèque at the time
was, according to Georges Sadoul, merely a "fragile fiction, a
bizarre magma." Langlois and Grémillon were members of the
French Cinema Liberation committee, and after Paris was lib-
erated Grémillon was the one who received famous visitors at

the offices on the avenue de Messine. In December 1944, for example, he welcomed Marlene Dietrich and Jean Gabin. He did not have much to do with the day-to-day running of the Cinémathèque or the Cercle du Cinéma, but he and Langlois were good friends, and his presence did much to enhance the growing prestige of the Cinémathèque.

At the end of the war, the Cercle du Cinéma resumed its weekly screenings at the little cinema opposite the Langlois apartment, the Studio de l'Étoile. Mary Meerson recalls that on V-E Day the film screened—by chance—was L'Age d'Or.

But now the demand for tickets exceeded the number of seats, and typically, Langlois selected those who could become members by giving them a questionnaire to see how much they knew—and therefore presumably cared—about the cinema. Alain Resnais tells me he managed to pass the test: the only question he can remember was "Who is Bertolt Brecht?" For most Frenchmen in 1945, Brecht, if known at all, was simply the author of The Threepenny Opera.

In 1946 the Cercle du Cinéma moved to a theater in the Musée Guimet, place d'Iéna. Interestingly enough—in light of Langlois's later views on the subject—the silent films at the Salle d'Iéna were accompanied by piano music played by no less a personage than Joseph Kosma (author of the scores for many films, such as Children of Paradise and Partie de Campagne, as well as of the song "Autumn Leaves"). Langlois, says Mary Meerson, scrupulously refrained from recording those brilliant piano improvisations—only to be told later by Kosma that he wished Langlois had recorded them, because he couldn't remember what he had played and could have used some of it for other purposes.

When Langlois could no longer afford to have piano accompaniment, he convinced himself that silent films shouldn't be played with music. This in spite of the fact that in com-

mercial cinemas there had always been accompaniments—
with orchestras in the first-run theaters, Wurlitzer organs in
second-run, and pianos in the rest. He made a virtue out of
necessity and built up a theory that the visual rhythm of the
silent film was sufficient in itself and could only be spoiled by
music.

Even before Langlois decided to convene a congress of
FIAF in Paris in 1946, he had already resumed his proselytiz-
ing efforts abroad. One of his exhibitions in Lausanne was in-
strumental in the establishment of the Cinémathèque Suisse,
according to Freddy Buache, its founder.

Langlois organized in Lausanne in 1945 a large exhibition
called "Images du Cinéma Français." "People like me,"
Buache wrote, "who were twenty years old and who had
grown up in a country surrounded by war, who were only able
to see German films, with no knowledge of the classics, were
almost completely ignorant of film history. We knew that Eisenstein existed, but we had never seen Potemkin. We knew
that Chien Andalou and L'Age d'Or existed, but they were
myths for us. So when Langlois organized this great exhibition at the Fine Arts Museum of Lausanne, along with screenings of extracts from some of these unknown films, I went
every day. I was interested in the cinema, and I could see at
the exhibition photos of Les Vampires, sets by Méliès, and a
lot of other things, from the wax head of Micheline Presle in
La Nuit Fantastique [Marcel L'Herbier] to the maquettes for
Children of Paradise. Finally, when I went into the little room
where extracts of films were being shown continuously, in
loops, I was thunderstruck by the revelation of films like Un
Chien Andalou, Entr'acte [René Clair] and Le Brasier Ardent
[Mozhukhin].

"I came out, my head in a whirl, and asked the first person
I saw, 'When do these films get shown again?' 'In an hour,' I

was told. So I went back over and over again. I talked to one
or two of the people there—Langlois and Jean Grémillon—
whose names didn't mean anything to me. Langlois was very
nice to me; we had dinner together and at night went to
screenings of French 'primitive' films. So it was from all this
that I got the idea, along with some friends, of creating a *cinémathèque* in Lausanne. There was a Swiss archive already, set
up in 1943 in the Basel Museum of Fine Arts. The idea was to
include film in the activities of the museum just as the Museum of Modern Art in New York had done. But it never came
to much, and eventually they agreed to give us the collection
of films they had amassed."[1]

By 1950 the Cinémathèque Suisse was officially inaugurated in Lausanne, where it still thrives under the direction of
the same Freddy Buache. His relationship with Langlois was
to have its ups and downs, but they often exchanged films,
and it was thanks to Buache that Langlois was always able to
show one of Max Ophüls's best films, *La Signora di Tutti*.

Langlois also continued to help the Cinémathèque de Belgique—again, independently of FIAF. In the words of André
Thirifays, "In 1945, after the war, I saw Langlois again, and
he persuaded me to revive our Cinémathèque, which already
existed legally but was not very active. In 1945 we had very
few films, and Langlois said, 'I'll lend you all the films you
want—that way you can show them, make a little money,
and build your Cinémathèque.' And it was his pressure that
gave new life to the Cinémathèque de Belgique. For a year,
Langlois sent us films constantly—we showed them in the Palais des Beaux Arts in Brussels in the large concert hall. I also
found films myself in Belgium that had not been destroyed by
the Germans. I bought some, but mostly they were given to
us. So by 1946 we had thirty films of real importance. And
then we were able to exchange with the other archives. Lan-

glois had made us members of FIAF in 1946. We got no money from the state until 1960.

"Langlois also mounted some prodigious exhibitions for us—Méliès and other pre–World War I directors, animated film—and then in 1949 we had our first experimental film festival in Knokke-le-Zoute. This show was organized by Langlois and Georges Sadoul, and by Jacques Ledoux, who had just joined us—he was a student at the time. Ledoux was Polish by origin, and his parents were executed in Brussels during the war, but he escaped. He was taken in by some Catholic monks, and he adopted the name of Ledoux. After the war he went back to the university, but he was already bitten by the cinema bug. Henri Storck [the Belgian documentary filmmaker] introduced him to me, saying he'd work for nothing at the Cinémathèque. That was in 1947. I was secretary-general, and we had fifteen employees. Over a period of years Langlois deposited over three hundred important films with us. At the beginning Ledoux liked Langlois very much. But Langlois knew that Ledoux had a very strong personality, so he became for him a potential adversary. And from being a potential adversary, Langlois made of him a real opponent."

All these agreements between the Cinémathèque Française and the new groups were bilateral. FIAF was a much more official, even bureaucratic affair. FIAF started its activities again when Langlois held the 1946 Congress in Paris, the first since the one in New York before the war. By this time Franju had had enough of both the Cinémathèque and FIAF, and resigned as secretary-general. Iris Barry replaced the absent Frank Hensel as president. (Franju's place was taken by Z. de Malewsky-Malevitch, who held the job until 1951; he was followed by Farrokh Gaffary, and in 1956 Mar-

ion Michelle took over the job.) The political climate was
such that, opportunistically, FIAF decided to make Gosfilmo-
fond—the Soviet Film Archive—a "retroactive" founder-
member, thus erasing almost all traces of Hensel and the
Reichsfilmarchiv. Franju had always wanted to make films, so
he joined the Scientific Film Institute, a government organization run by director Jean Painlevé. During his seven-year
stay there he directed his first important shorts: *Le Sang des
Bêtes*, *Hôtel des Invalides*, and *Monsieur et Madame Curie*.

After Lotte Eisner returned to the Cinémathèque and became its curator, she began to collect the objects—costumes,
sets, stills, drawings—that would be used for Langlois's small
exhibitions. Although there were no screenings yet at the avenue de Messine, the offices were there, and there Langlois
put on shows of costumes, posters, and set designs: in 1945,
"Images du Cinéma Français"; and in 1946, the works of
Émile Reynaud, the important French "primitive."

The Cercle du Cinéma was too small, too select a forum for
all the films Langlois wanted to show: there were neither
enough seats nor enough screenings. In 1947 it gave way to
the Cinémathèque Française as an organization which not
only preserved films but screened them on its own premises.
The small theater constructed by the Germans was adapted
for this purpose. And that is how a small *hôtel particulier* on
the avenue de Messine, diagonally across from the Galerie
Maeght, then the most important modern art gallery in Paris,
became the most important film theater in the world.

The year 1948 was an important one. First of all, Langlois
inaugurated a museum, the Musée Permanent du Cinéma, on the avenue de Messine, along with its screening
room—about fifty seats. Then, as after, his legal fiction was

that one bought a ticket to see the museum, and then paid one old franc extra to see the film—thus enabling the Cinémathèque to function not as a cinema but as a museum. In 1948 he also got the government to donate part of the abandoned fort of Bois d'Arcy—in the suburbs of Paris—for the Cinémathèque to store its films.

Janet Flanner (Genêt) has given an evocative description of the atmosphere of the avenue de Messine:

> The mysterious magic lantern atmosphere of its shabby foyer—a tortuous black little maze, illuminated by lights that shine through and give form to the images on the strips of movie film decorating its walls. Another feature of its decor is a startling life-size blow-up of a white-capped man, dressed in white tights, who has one foot lifted—the anonymous "Walking Man." This and "Flying Birds" are thought by many to be the first true motion pictures; they were taken in 1888 by the French physiologist Étienne [-Jules] Marey with his synthesizing photography gun, which looks vaguely like any gun to kill people or birds with and is also on display in the shadowy foyer. . . . It also possesses the first example of today's animated cartoons: lovely little hand-painted pictures of jugglers and top-hatted Amazons, shown on the Paris boulevards in 1892 by means of the rotating praxinoscope, invented by the tragically ill-rewarded artist Emile Reynaud.[2]

The little theater on the avenue de Messine began by showing a repeating cycle of "100 Masterpieces." Only one film was shown per night, but it was projected twice. Later, this would change to the familiar rhythm of three different films a night—6:30, 8:30, 10:30.

Now that the Cinémathèque was open to anyone who could get in, it became the center for a group of young men—

later called Children of the Cinémathèque—who were to form their own film clubs, to become film critics, mostly for *Cahiers du Cinéma*, and then to make films. They were François Truffaut, Jean-Luc Godard, Eric Rohmer, Jacques Rivette, and Claude Chabrol—the godchildren of Henri Langlois.

"Up to 1934," Langlois has reminded us, "a young man of twenty living in Paris could have seen almost all the great films that had ever been made, since it was sufficient for him to have frequented neighborhood theaters in his childhood and adolescence to have caught up with the films made before he was born."[3] As Eric Rohmer later remarked: "Can you imagine a budding musician who was unable to listen to the works of Bach or Beethoven, a young writer who was not able to read the works of the past by going to a library? So by what right is the budding filmmaker (or film critic) denied the same rights?"[4] Furthermore, because of the war, many American and foreign films were unknown to a whole generation of *cinéphiles*.

"For the cinema to have a future," said Rohmer, "its past could not be allowed to die."[5] And in the screening room of the avenue de Messine, this young generation devoured the films of the past: silent films and talkies, German expressionist and Italian neorealist films, experimental films. "Here," as Annette Insdorf put it, "they learned to love directors like Howard Hawks and John Ford. . . . The Cinémathèque made them aware and enamored of genres: Westerns, musicals, gangster films, 'film noir'—and of the Hollywood studio system; the genre conventions and production methods were seen as necessary limitations that defined the possibilities of personal expression for American directors. Paradoxically enough, their limited knowledge of English made them uniquely equipped to appreciate individual cinematic style:

the American films often had no subtitles, thereby inviting a closer look at how movement is expressed through visual texture, composition, camera movement, and editing."[6]

Moreover, as Eric Rhode has pointed out, it was not only the number of films they were able to see—it was the way they were programmed. "[Langlois] would run three films every evening in unexpected yet revealing juxtapositions, placing an Eisenstein before a Raoul Walsh, or a Hitchcock after a Mizoguchi. Those who were regular members of his audience were among the first to have their sensibilities immersed in the history of images from the time of [Eadweard] Muybridge and Marey onwards. . . ."[7]

François Truffaut's first encounter with Langlois, he told me, "was not actually at the Cinémathèque itself, but at a screening put on by the Cinémathèque at the Lycée Montaigne on a Sunday afternoon. I must have seen an ad for it in the *Écran Français*—that's the only way I could have known about it. I seem to remember it was a screening of some Griffith shorts—*The New York Hat*, for example. I even think that that was the first time I ever saw André Bazin [Truffaut's mentor and father figure, and the most important film theorist of his time]. But I can't be sure—there were so many things happening at once then, all kinds of *ciné-clubs*. Anyhow, when I first saw Langlois, I thought he looked like Robert Newton in *Odd Man Out*. As for the avenue de Messine, I first started going there in, probably, 1947 [but it must have been 1948], and it was there that we all met—Rivette, Jean-Luc, a Polish-born girl called Liliane, Suzanne Schiffman, and a Swedish girl whose name I can't remember. We always met there. My first surprise at the avenue de Messine was that sometimes the screenings ended very late, after the last metro, so one had to walk home. I would go see a film called *Birth of a Nation* without realizing how long it was. Actually, I did have contact with Langlois in 1948—correspondence. I had

written to ask him to let my *ciné-club* borrow prints of
Entr'acte, *Un Chien Andalou*, and Cocteau's *The Blood of a
Poet*. He answered that we could show the first two, but
claimed he had no print of the Cocteau film.

"At the avenue de Messine, I didn't see too much of Langlois: the person we saw most was Frédéric Rossif [who was
later to become a filmmaker, too: *To Die in Madrid* and other
montage films], because it was he who tore the tickets at the
entrance. He was a threatening figure for us, because we tried
to stay inside between screenings so as not to have to pay for
the next one. Musidora, the silent-film star, was always there
too, at the entrance, and Lotte Eisner, but I don't remember
seeing Mary Meerson."

Truffaut talked to Langlois only once in those early days. "I
was leaving for the army (I volunteered in 1950), and I went
and asked Langlois whether, if I gave the Cinémathèque my
files, would he let me in free to the screenings after I came
back from the army. He said yes, so I rented a cart, and
brought all my 'treasures' to the Cinémathèque. They weren't
particularly valuable—stupid press cuttings and a lot of stills I
had stolen from cinemas.

"The Cinémathèque was really a haven for us then, a refuge, our home, everything. There were only about fifty seats,
and we had the habit of not sitting down, but of lying on the
floor in front of the first row of seats—especially for the popular films. Langlois used to reproach the audience for coming
only to the popular films, the classics, and he was right. I remember films like *Kühle Wampe* [directed by Slatan Dudow,
script by Bertolt Brecht] where there were only five or six
people in the theater.

"Langlois and Bazin were not great friends, you know.
Langlois didn't have too much respect for critics. You can tell
that when you read his own texts. They're very much like
conversation . . . although often very apt. But Bazin's intelli-

gence was more Sartrean, acutely reasoned. Sometimes his arguments had little to do with the actual film he was writing about. I think Langlois didn't like the professorial side of Bazin. Bazin was a professor, he was a proselytizer, and he was didactic. And Henri must have been against all that. He wanted to show films and let it go at that.

"He believed in education by osmosis, and I felt that way, too. But Bazin liked the Cinémathèque and he liked Langlois. And Bazin went to the Cinémathèque all the time. I must admit now that, looking back, I used to behave quite badly at the avenue de Messine. I used to try to get in without paying; I used to smoke during the screenings; and I used to try to see three screenings for the price of one.

"In those days my judgment of films was very fluctuating, so I depended a lot on Rivette, who was a great influence on me. I was impressed by everything I saw in those early days—the films were like a drug for me. And seeing silent films for the first time was a great shock. The first films I remember really liking sincerely were Vigo's. I didn't need anyone's advice or persuasion for them, whereas I never in those days had a very precise judgment on silent films.

"At the Cinémathèque I used to always listen to what everyone else said—the conversations on the way out of the cinema. When I got out of the army, I went back to the avenue de Messine, and began to write in Cahiers du Cinéma, and Arts-Spectacles, and then I really came to know Langlois."

Jacques Rivette expressed his debt to Langlois similarly: "I remember the avenue de Messine with its fifty seats, which were full only for L'Age d'Or, The Blue Angel, or Potemkin, but were practically empty for the films of Griffith, Stiller, and Murnau. At the end of 1949 I was a young man from the provinces, and it was there I met Truffaut and Godard—at those screenings when there were only five or six people in the theater."

Children of the Cinémathèque

And Godard said that "but for his titanic efforts, the history of the cinema would have remained what it was for Bardèche and Brasillach [writers of the first French film history, *Histoire du Cinéma*, in 1935, later translated into English by Iris Barry]—souvenir postcards brought back by a pair of amiable but not very serious students from the land of darkened auditoriums.

"One can see immediately the revolution that might be effected in the aesthetic of moving pictures by this new vision of historicity . . . I will simply say that, thanks to Henri Langlois, we now know—to choose at random—that ceilings do not date from *Citizen Kane* but from Griffith (of course) and Gance; cinema verité, not from Rouch but John Ford; and the camerawork of *Metropolis* from an anonymous French cameraman, [Félix Mesguisch], contemporary with the academic salon painter Bouguereau. We know, too, that Alain Resnais and Otto Preminger have not progressed beyond Lumière, Griffith, and Dreyer, any more than Cézanne and Braque progressed beyond David and Chardin: they did something different. Henri Langlois has given each twenty-fourth of a second* of his life to rescue all these voices from the silent obscurity and to project them on the white sky of the only museum where the real and imaginary** meet at last."[8]

Although Langlois always claimed that he was not a teacher, that he had no didactic aims in view in programming the Cinémathèque, this was not quite true. He wanted to share his enthusiasm with as many people as possible, and by showing films that had not been seen for many years, he changed our ideas of film history. In the forties and

---

*Sound films run at twenty-four frames per second.
**A reference to André Malraux's *The Imaginary Museum*.

early fifties he rediscovered Feuillade and broadened our knowledge of the genius of Erich von Stroheim.

As Alain Resnais put it, "Like thousands of other people, I owe my discovery of Feuillade to Henri Langlois, who can never be thanked enough. I knew Feuillade's name, of course, but had it not been for the screening in 1945 at the Cinémathèque [actually the Cercle du Cinéma], I would never have become conscious of Feuillade's greatness. This discovery knocked me for a loop, for it taught me that the films that I had long dreamed of actually existed."

That Griffith was admired and Feuillade disdained during their lifetimes should not surprise us. The most successful playwrights of the nineteenth century are not always those who are revived today. It was difficult for critics of the twenties to separate Feuillade from the other, less talented directors of melodramas; to judge, one needs time. The French were able to appreciate Griffith immediately only because he was exotic for them—separation by space served the function of separation in time.

After all, was not Feuillade just a maker of serials? Weren't they just melodramas? The leading lights, the avant-garde, were deceived both by the popular nature of the subject matter and by Feuillade's own declaration that he was "just an artisan."

These serials, by the way, were different from the kind most Americans grew up on in the thirties. They were not twenty-minute episodes which ended in cliff-hangers: they were hour-long episodes, each more or less complete in itself, but with a story that threaded its way through ten or twelve episodes. Langlois was the first to show all the episodes strung together, making up programs of about six hours.

Langlois said that he himself discovered Feuillade only in 1936; at that time, he was considered a dreadful filmmaker.

Children of the Cinémathèque

"By chance I happened to see *Fantômas* (1913), and I found it superb. Behind consecrated values, there were other values—not yet consecrated—and which were revealed to be also of importance."[9]

But, to be accurate, the films *had* been admired in the 1920s by the Surrealists: Louis Aragon, André Breton, and Luis Buñuel; they felt an affinity for Feuillade's technique of situating bizarre adventures against everyday backgrounds. Buñuel once told Sadoul how much he preferred *Fantômas* and *Les Vampires* to the avant-garde films of the twenties—which he loathed. But ironically, Sadoul tells us, Buñuel didn't even know the name of the director of these films. So if the Surrealists (whom Langlois admired) were the real discoverers of *Les Vampires*, it was Langlois who saved Feuillade for posterity, who *imposed* him, not only as a great figure of the past, but as a precursor of a future cinema, an influence and an inspiration.

The rediscovery of Feuillade had a double effect: on the one hand, it rewrote cinema history, for Feuillade was a forgotten figure in France and was unknown in Great Britain and America. The other effect was Feuillade's influence on directors like Resnais, Franju, and Rivette, whose original thirteen-hour version of *Out One* especially seems to show that influence. Up to 1944, it had often been said that the French cinema had two traditions—Méliès and Lumière, fantasy and reality, or what you will. But Feuillade became, as Francis Lacassin put it, the Third Man, and filmmakers were struck by the mixture of realism and surrealism in his work.

Musidora, who had starred as Irma Vep* in *Les Vampires*, worked for the Cinémathèque: in theory she was supposed to devote her time to collecting costumes, but like everyone else

---

*An anagram of "vampire."

there, she did whatever Langlois needed done at any given moment. For a long time it was she—taking over from Langlois's mother—who sold tickets at the box office. But Alain Resnais remembers the evening when she presented in person *Les Vampires*, that 1915 film which many, including André Bazin, consider to be one of the greatest of all time.

In one of his essays Bazin recounts a Cinémathèque screening:

> That night only one of the two projectors was working. In addition, the print had no intertitles. . . . The fact that the lights had to be turned on every fifteen minutes to change reels seemed to multiply the episodes. Seen under these conditions, Feuillade's masterpiece reveals the aesthetic principle that lies behind its charm. Every interruption evoked an "ah" of disappointment, and every fresh start a sigh of hope for solution. The story held our attention and carried us along purely and simply by the tension created in the telling. There was no question of pre-existing action broken up by intervals . . . the unbearable tension set up by the next episode to follow and the anxious wait [were] not so much for the events to come as for the continuation of the telling, of the re-starting of an interrupted act of creation. Feuillade himself proceeded in the same way in making his films. He had no idea of what would happen next, and filmed step-by-step as the morning's inspiration came. Both the author and the spectator were in the same situation, namely that of the King and Scheherazade, the repeated intervals of darkness in the cinema paralleling the separating off of the Thousand and One Nights.[10]

F inding, preserving, and showing films were not Langlois's only aims. Whenever it was possible, he tried to restore films to their original state. The most spectacular of these restorations was the sound print of Erich von Stroheim's 1927 *The Wedding March*. Stroheim's reputation as a director had always been higher in France than in America or Britain. Indeed, when Gavin Lambert, then editor of *Sight and Sound*, wrote his 1953 groundbreaking piece, "Stroheim Revisited: The Missing Third in the American Cinema," there was no print of a Stroheim film in preservation in Great Britain. Lambert had gone to Paris to see *The Wedding March*. The results of that visit and of screenings of Stroheim films organized by Olwen Vaughan at the New London Film Society convinced him that "time will restore Stroheim to his place as the missing third of the American cinema, along with Griffith and Chaplin, in the golden age—the twenty years between 1915 and 1935 when producers (sometimes to their cost) were more adventurous and censors more liberal. . . ." And he added that "*The Wedding March* is a more substantial film than *Foolish Wives* and it seems now, in many ways, the richest of all Stroheim's work. Its picture of a collapsing aristocracy is more powerful and complex, there is a solid grandeur about it."[11]

Langlois had first met Stroheim a few years before the outbreak of World War II. He had gone with Lotte Eisner and a few journalists to see Stroheim during his visit to Paris. "They gave me a knockout blow in Hollywood," Stroheim said bitterly, "and I'm still a little groggy." That is how Lotte Eisner remembered his first words to them.[12] She and Langlois wished they had had enough money to enable him to make a new film. This was impossible then, as it would be later, but just as Langlois dreamed of recovering the negative of Eisenstein's *Que Viva Mexico!* and inviting Eisenstein to put it together, so he dreamed of restoring the mutilated prints of Stroheim's films, almost none of which had ever been shown complete.

Years later, in the early fifties, when Stroheim had settled in France, they were able to show him his films in their theater on the avenue de Messine. It was the first time he had ever seen a release print of his 1924 *Greed*, which had been cut by nearly two thirds, and he was horrified. In 1953 they showed him *The Wedding March*. After a few minutes he stood up and said, "This is unbearable, boring, horrible." Lotte Eisner looked at him, outraged at his sacrilege. Stroheim asked at what speed it was being projected. "At the proper silent speed," they proudly announced. "Sixteen frames per second." "But we shot it at sound speed," he said, "twenty-four frames a second—there was music, on records, to accompany it."*

Neither Langlois nor Eisner knew that the film originally had synchronized music on disks, because it was shown that way only in America. The print they showed Stroheim had been acquired by Thomas Quinn Curtis from the estate of Patrick Powers, producer of the film for Paramount. Then late in 1953, a friend of Curtis's, Russell Holman of Paramount, who happened to be in Paris, promised Curtis (a longtime friend and benefactor of Stroheim's) that he would find the records and send them to Paris. Which in due course he did. And somehow Langlois managed to find the money to finance the transfer from disks to film.

The actual job was done by the well-known editor Renée

---

*Although early silent films were meant to be screened at sixteen frames per second—if they are not, they look ridiculously jerky—by the time of the coming of sound there was a tremendous variation in the speeds of films, so that some are best seen at eighteen frames per second, others at twenty-two or twenty-four; sometimes it is even necessary to vary the speed during the course of a film. When sound came in, the speed for shooting was fixed internationally at twenty-four frames per second and has remained so (except for television, which shows films at twenty-five frames per second).

Children of the Cinémathèque

Lichtig, together with Stroheim. The whole job had to be fin-ished in a week because the film was to be shown at the São Paulo Festival in Brazil; so, as always at the Cinémathèque, the job was completed by working through the night. As Lichtig described the task,[13] the first step was to record the music on tape; then it was carefully synchronized—for there was not only music on those $33\frac{1}{3}$ rpm disks but also the occa-sional sound effect. But because the original print had shrunk slightly with the passage of time, there was often a three- or four-second discrepancy per reel. So a little cheating was nec-essary; fortunately Stroheim was there and he was able to find a solution to each problem.

The sound version was a triumph at São Paulo. André Ba-zin reported: "*The Wedding March* was a sound film, and we had forgotten that. Not only did this reconstruction restore the work to its true aesthetic speed, its own dramatic timing, but it showed once more how vain is the traditional opposi-tion of the silent film and the sound film, as well as the sup-position that there was a radical break between these two periods of the cinema."* [14]

Langlois lent this print to the National Film Theatre in London in 1963 for the program called "School of Vienna,"

---

*Perhaps because of this sound version, *The Wedding March* was chosen over *Greed* when *Cahiers du Cinéma* published its top twelve greatest films in 1958. The voting was, typically, first done by director; then a film by that director was chosen. The voters included, among the *Ca-hiers* team, Bazin, Chabrol, Godard, Rivette, Rohmer, and Truffaut. The twelve were, in *Cahiers's* preferential order: (1) *Sunrise*; (2) *Rules of the Game*; (3) *Journey to Italy* (also called *Strangers*, by Ros-sellini); (4) *Ivan the Terrible*; (5) *Birth of a Nation*; (6) Welles's *Confi-dential Report* (also known as *Mr. Arkadin*); (7) Dreyer's *Ordet*; (8) *Ugetsu*; (9) *L'Atalante*; (10) *The Wedding March*; (11) Hitchcock's *Under Capricorn*; and (12) *Monsieur Verdoux*—all films constantly shown at the Cinémathèque.

and later to the New York Film Festival, and in both places audiences and critics found it something of a revelation. Until then American audiences knew Stroheim only from the extremely mutilated *Greed* and *Foolish Wives*.

Alas, the story does not end here. For *The Wedding March* was originally meant to have been a much longer film. It was to make up a three-hour program, thus leaving no room for the usual second feature; Stroheim detested the idea of a double bill. But as soon as he had shaped the first half of the film—what we now know as *The Wedding March*—the second part was taken out of his hands and entrusted, as Lotte Eisner puts it, to Stroheim's great rival, Josef von Sternberg. Sternberg, following studio instructions, made a film which could be shown independently: *The Honeymoon*. But since it would not make much sense to anyone who had not seen *The Wedding March*, Sternberg concocted a prologue from sequences in *The Wedding March*. *The Honeymoon* was never shown in America, but was given a limited European release.

According to Eisner, the "digest" introduction irreparably damaged the rhythm of the film, but *The Honeymoon* did contain one unforgettable scene: "The wedding night of the prince (Stroheim) and the beautiful lame daughter (ZaSu Pitts) of the corn-plaster magnate whom the prince has been forced to marry. Here Stroheim revealed the curious mixture of aversion and attraction felt by the prince towards his bride."

According to those who saw it, *The Honeymoon* (known in France as *Mariage de Prince*) was only a shadow of a shadow. The Cinémathèque did possess a print of it—apparently the only one in existence—until 1959. It was stacked in the courtyard of the Cinémathèque building, rue de Courcelles, awaiting transit on a hot summer's day. The courtyard was partially covered with an iron-and-glass marquee, and that,

we are told, was the cause of the fire that broke out in the
summer of 1959. No one, I think, to this day knows just how
many films perished in that fire, but *The Honeymoon* was one
of them.

Some archivists doubted whether the fire actually ever took
place—as if it had been a fake, a plot by Langlois to *pretend*
that some films had been burned so he could hang on to
them. I was in Paris at the time and can testify to the fire: I
read about it in the newspaper early on the morning after it
happened, and went to the Cinémathèque to offer condo-
lences. The smell was still in the air, and Langlois was half
crazed. It was probably grief, but it came out in paranoid fury;
he thought, or pretended to think, that I had come to sneer,
to crow over his misfortune. "Go on," he yelled, his face and
clothes smudged with soot from cleaning up the wreckage,
"go back to the British Film Institute and tell them—they'll
be glad to hear the news."

But this rage lasted only a few minutes, and he calmed
down and let me in to survey the gruesome scene. Was Langlois "to blame" for the loss of *The Honeymoon*? Yes and no.
No, because fires have broken out on the best-run archives—
there have been several in the United States in the past few
years. Yes, because in a well-run archive, films would not be
piled up in an open courtyard on a hot day. But the Cinémathèque couldn't be well ordered because Langlois was always
trying to do more than was humanly or financially possible.
"Well-run" archives refuse to take more films than they can
"properly" take care of. "Well-run" archives would never allow a unique print out of the vaults, would never show it at
all except on a Moviola or a similar viewing machine.

On the other hand, none of the well-run archives ever
thought of restoring the original sound to *The Wedding March*.
No other archivist would have inspired people like Thomas

Quinn Curtis or, indeed, Stroheim himself to give him the necessary material to do the job. Langlois's defects were the other side of the coin of his qualities.

Langlois made amends to Stroheim, as it were, later, by obtaining two reels of the "African footage" of Stroheim's *Queen Kelly*. This film, produced by Joseph P. Kennedy for Gloria Swanson, was interrupted by the coming of sound. That, added to the mounting costs of the shooting, seemed to Mr. Kennedy to make the film not worth finishing. Stroheim was removed from the film before the production was completed, and his eleven-reel version was reduced to eight, reportedly by Miss Swanson herself. *Queen Kelly* was never released in the United States, but it was shown in Europe. From the stills, Langlois knew that although Miss Swanson's release print ends with Kelly's apparent suicide (a scene directed by Miss Swanson), some of the later part of the story was filmed.

Langlois was not the only one who knew this, of course. In an interview with Richard Griffith, then director of the film department of the Museum of Modern Art in New York, Herman G. Weinberg asked Griffith whether he had ever found any traces of the African sequences of *Queen Kelly*. "Yes," Griffith replied, "a little over a year ago, Dudley Murphy told me he had some of the material and promised it to us." "Why haven't you got it yet?" asked Weinberg. "Pure negligence," replied Griffith, "I was too busy to chase Dudley up about it."[15] Neither he nor anyone at the museum ever did "find the time" to chase Dudley up about it, and now he is dead.* Lan-

---

*Dudley Murphy was a strange, marginal character. His career, as far as I can make out, began when he photographed (and, according to some sources, co-directed) the painter Fernand Léger's film *Ballet Mecanique* in the early 1920s. Later, he made many films in Hollywood—most of

Children of the Cinémathèque

glois, of course, did get those extraordinary two reels from Mr. Murphy. Kelly (whose suicide turns out to have been unsuccessful) is called away to Africa by a telegram from her guardian aunt. The aunt operates a brothel in German East Africa, and on her deathbed forces Kelly to marry a degenerate drunken cripple. As anyone who knows Stroheim's work can imagine, it is a beautifully baroque and powerful sequence. Langlois lent it to the National Film Theatre in London in February 1965, where it was greatly appreciated. These twenty minutes don't entirely make up for the loss of *The Honeymoon*, but they go some way in that direction.

---

which sound like potboilers—*Confessions of a Co-ed* (1931), *The Sport Parade* (1932), and others. But there were two more remarkable films— *The Emperor Jones*, starring Paul Robeson, in 1933, and in 1939, *One Third of a Nation*.

6

Crossing the Seine

During the late forties and early fifties, Langlois's activities expanded far beyond the avenue de Messine. At the same time, and not coincidentally, there began a concerted attempt to create a new kind of film culture in France. The first important event was the 1949 Biarritz Festival du Film Maudit (literally "damned" or "cursed" films, but figuratively films that had been kept from release or had not received proper attention). According to Mary Meerson, the festival was Langlois's idea. When he approached Jean Cocteau to convince him that something must be done for the "*film maudit,*" Cocteau came back with "Give me that as a title and I'll find a way of doing something about it." Langlois and Cocteau were members of the jury, which also included Bresson, René Clément, Alexandre Astruc, Roger Leenhardt, Jean Grémillon, Jean-Georges Auriol, François Mauriac, and Raymond Queneau.

It was what we could now call an "alternative" festival—alternative to Cannes. The Cannes Film Festival, which itself had first been planned in the late thirties as an "alternative" to the Fascist-dominated Venice Festival—then the only film festival in the world—was supposed to have started on September 1, 1939. The war intervened, and the first festival was not held until 1946. Curiously enough, both the municipalities of Cannes and Biarritz had been contenders for the "free-world" festival in 1939; Biarritz lost out.

The Festival du Film Maudit had a great impact on film criticism in France, and according to Dudley Andrew[1] might be said to have been the first success of a movement toward the personal cinema of auteurs which would culminate in the New Wave ten years later. The choice of films was eclectic: Bresson's *Les Dames du Bois de Boulogne*, Grémillon's *Lumière d'Eté*, Ford's *The Long Voyage Home*, and the first screening of Vigo's *L'Atalante* in its restored integral version. There were new films, too: *Jour de Fête* by Jacques Tati, Orson Welles's *The Lady from Shanghai.*

The festival was a success, and was followed in 1950 by a second edition. But in spite of the French premiere of Michelangelo Antonioni's first feature, *Cronaca di un Amore*, as well as of Nicholas Ray's first film, *They Live by Night*, the second, and last, Biarritz festival was a failure. The novelty was gone, Cocteau did not take part, and many complained that the program concentrated too heavily on new British films which, although good, did not fit into the category of *film maudit.* Indeed, one could scarcely use that term to describe *The Thirty-nine Steps, Tight Little Island,* (original title: *Whisky Galore*), or *Major Barbara.*

Another reason for its failure was the fact that the important French film magazine *La Revue du Cinéma,* which had strongly backed Biarritz, had gone out of business just after the first festival. A replacement of a sort came out in 1950, the short-lived *Gazette du Cinéma.* It was only an eight-page tabloid, but it was edited by Eric Rohmer, and its articles were signed by Jacques Rivette and Jean-Luc Godard, so it was a link between the prestigious glossy *Revue du Cinéma* (which had been published by Gallimard, the most important French publisher) and *Cahiers du Cinéma.*

The *Cahiers du Cinéma* first appeared in April 1951: it had a yellow cover like *La Revue du Cinéma,* and Jacques Doniol-Valcroze, who had been an associate editor of *La Revue* became, with André Bazin and Lo Duca, an editor-in-chief of *Cahiers.* Many of the writers for *La Revue* continued to write for *Cahiers:* Bazin, Lotte Eisner, and Langlois himself. But Bazin soon gathered round him some younger critics: Truffaut, Godard, Rohmer, Rivette, and Chabrol. And over the years, *Cahiers* and the Cinémathèque were to have a fruitfully symbiotic relationship.

If the organizers of Biarritz were discouraged, Langlois was not: he decided to have his "own" festival in the Riviera town of Antibes. As Biarritz had been an "alternative" to Cannes, so Antibes was to be an "alternative" to Biarritz. It was a success, according to Arthur Knight, who spent two weeks with Langlois in Antibes. "Delirious" was the word he used, and he meant it literally. "Langlois," wrote Knight,

> had organized (if that's the word) a film festival in that gracious city and—intentionally, I'm certain—managed to

shake up just about everyone there. In the open market place where films were shown free to the local citizenry, he tended to run the most recherché, the most esoteric, and most avant-garde films that he could lay his hands on (although I must admit that it was also there that I saw Abel Gance's two-hour *La Roue*—standing). In the city-owned fortress, where wealthier residents and visiting dignitaries could pay for seats, he ran *L'Age d'Or*. And at the festival's one proper theater, where retrospectives of Warner Bros. and John Huston films were shown, the performances never started on time (generally late, but what was worse, occasionally early . . .) and rarely was the film that was shown the one that had been announced. When asked for advance information about his programs, Langlois would smile a secret smile, hold up one finger, and say "Wait. It is a surprise." He never wanted anyone to take his movies for granted.[2]

Langlois added a curious note to the festival by commissioning a number of 16 mm films (and one in 35 mm) by writers and artists. The Cinémathèque gave them the raw stock and a technical adviser, and let them do what they wanted. The most famous of these—and indeed the only one that seems to have survived—was Jean Genêt's *Un Chant d'Amour*. Jacques Rivette remembers there was also a short film by Sartre on graffiti, and one by Raymond Queneau called *En Passant*. Picasso began a film for Antibes, but it was never finished: all the footage was returned to him in the late fifties and has since disappeared.

But great success though some thought Antibes to be, it was never repeated. There were plans, but they never came to anything. And through all the years I knew Langlois—especially when we would sometimes leave the Cannes Festival to have lunch in his favorite restaurant in Antibes—he used to say to me, "Ah, if only you had been in Antibes in 1950. That was a festival; that was something you would never have forgotten." That same year Langlois began organizing retrospectives for the Cannes Film Festival; later he did the same for the Venice Festival.

In 1953 Langlois organized for Cannes an homage to the recently deceased Jean Epstein. Outside France, Epstein is remembered, if at all, for his expressionistic silent film version of *The Fall of the House of Usher* (1928). But he was also one of the great film theorists of the twenties, and his films included *Coeur Fidèle*, with its "lyrical montage," the still fascinating *Glace à Trois Faces* (1927), a kind of precursor to *Last Year at Marienbad*, as well as some starkly realistic studies of the life of Breton fishermen: *Mor'Vran* and *Finis Terrae*.

Not coincidentally, Epstein's sister Marie began to work at the Cinémathèque the following year, where her role, though unpublicized, was almost equal in importance to those of Lotte Eisner and Mary Meerson. Marie Epstein was born in 1899 in Warsaw of a French father and a Polish mother. She began working in the cinema by writing scripts for her brother. Then from 1927 to 1940 she was the collaborator of Jean Benoît-Lévy, with whom she codirected such well-known films as *La Maternelle* and *La Mort du Cygne* (*Ballerina* was the American title of this film; its Hollywood remake was called *The Unfinished Dance*).

She first met Langlois, she told me, when Benoît-Lévy's office was just across the street from the Langlois family's flat in the rue Troyon, and Langlois often came to discuss Benoît-Lévy's films as well as those of Jean Epstein. He was timid, she said, and thin as a string bean. He was never a close friend of Jean Epstein's, but it was he who saved all the Epstein films from destruction during the war, both negatives and positives. Marie worked for the Red Cross in the Unoccupied Zone, and she remembers Langlois's visit to her in Vichy when he promised that all her brother's films would be saved—and that they would be shown. From 1948 to 1951 Marie again collaborated with Benoît-Lévy on a series of television films on dance. After her brother died in 1953 Langlois asked her to come to work at the Cinémathèque. Her official post was as the head of the technical service, and she supervised the mounting and printing of films. This often required her to "cannibalize" several incomplete prints of an old film in order to achieve one complete or nearly complete version. It was she who, with Marcel L'Herbier, reconstituted the original version of his *L'Inhumaine*.

And if you wanted to borrow a print from the Cinémathèque, it was Marie you depended upon ultimately; often she alone knew exactly where everything was and in what state. She was therefore extremely precious to Langlois. Which doesn't mean that they didn't fight. They had screaming matches, but, tiny and frail as she is, slightly stooped, she always held her ground. She didn't always agree with Langlois. "He liked Feuillade a lot; I didn't. I was part of the first French avant-garde, and we reacted violently against Feuillade."

Marie Epstein came to the Cinémathèque at one of its most critical moments. In December 1950 the French government had passed a law which would make it eventually illegal to show, transport, or even possess nitrate films. This, to Langlois, was a great tragedy. The first fifty-five years of film history were on nitrate cellulose stock. It is of course highly inflammable; it is also visually superior to the acetate stock that has been used since the early fifties. André Malraux once proclaimed that even if the *Mona Lisa* were painted on dynamite, he would preserve it. Langlois felt the same way about nitrate. "He loved nitrate," Kenneth Anger told me. "For him it was a living, breathing thing that could die of neglect."

According to scientists, there is no way of preventing nitrate film from going unstable; it gives off noxious gases which can explode, it can become sticky, or it can turn into a mass of noxious goo. Langlois realized these dangers, and he knew of the famous Charity Bazaar fire at a film show in Paris in 1897 which killed 117 aristocrats in ten minutes. There have been other fires in theaters since then, of course, but somehow the world made do with nitrate for fifty-five years; if one was careful, Langlois said, there was no great danger.

Why did the government pass this law? Simple, explained Langlois. "It's all part of a 'plot' by two of the major film manufacturers, Eastman Kodak and Agfa." At first hearing, I thought, "More of Langlois's paranoia." It is true, of course, that the makers of acetate film stood to benefit greatly from a law which would make all archives and film companies transfer their nitrate prints onto acetate. Since nobody really knows just how long nitrate will last, or how long any individual prints will last, it is possible that film manufacturers took the more pessimistic view—if, that is, they had in any way lobbied for the ban on nitrate.

Certainly most other archivists were in favor of transferring their nitrate films onto acetate as soon as possible. And some of them were actually throwing away the originals as being too dangerous to store. This, to Langlois, was criminal. Couldn't they see how infinitely more beautiful the nitrate prints were when projected? Most of them couldn't. And some, like Ernest Lindgren of the British National Film Archive, had an almost pathological loathing of nitrate. Systematically, Lindgren would have his staff punch bits out of nitrate film and subject the bits to the "artificial aging test" (using red alizarin dye); if the film didn't pass the test, he would often offer it to any archive that could use it. But the test was not accurate: an archivist told me about a nitrate print of a film, William S. Hart's *Blue Blazes Rawden*, that he got from Lindgren because it was "going unstable," and twenty years later he was still projecting it.

This might make one almost believe in Langlois's unscientific views. Since nitrate film was, for him, alive, it could die in its cans. Taking the film out of the cans and projecting it, or at least rewinding it, protected it. The state of nitrate film depends on many imponderables—how the film was developed, the actual film stock—which varied over fifty-five years; so Langlois's methods of preservation varied also. When the original tinted print of Renoir's first feature, *La Fille de l'Eau*, started to become sticky, he hung it up with clothespins, like washing on a line, and after a few days the stickiness went, and the print is still in good condition.

David Robinson, critic and collector, said that he believed Langlois had a point: in his own experience of preserving film posters, he found that if you leave them in neat piles they rot, but if you use them, they don't. Langlois explained his practice by analogy: it is an established fact that pearls will lose their luster if they are not worn. On the other hand, as the Yiddish proverb goes, "For example is no proof."

Perhaps because it was impossible to prove the argument for or against transfer to acetate, nitrate film became Langlois's favorite topic for years. "Whenever there was a lull in the conversation," Elliott Stein told me, "instead of making some remark about the weather as most people do, Langlois would start talking about nitrate. It was his *bête noire*—he always had in his mind the fear that the antinitrate forces were closing in on him."

The antinitrate law was going to help the Cinémathèque, however, because it was the only organization in France that was allowed to preserve nitrate. Several deadlines had been set: anyone in possession of a nitrate work print could keep it until January 1, 1951; March 1, 1951, was the expiration date for trailers on nitrate; June 1 for French prints in distribution, etc. So the labs and the copyright holders had enormous stocks of film either to destroy or give to the Cinémathèque. Many of them chose the Cinémathèque, and for months truckloads of film would arrive at its storage vault in Bois d'Arcy. So many arrived at once, in fact, that there was no way of sorting the films according to their physical condition. Nor would the Cinémathèque refuse to take a film because of its condition. "Some of the films were already in a state of decomposition," Marie Epstein told me, "and it would have taken an army to deal with all that material. We did the best we could with the means we had at our disposition."

This was confirmed to me by two former employees of the Cinémathèque who are not entirely uncritical of Langlois— Georges Goldfayn and Bernard Martinand. As Goldfayn said, "The films that arrived often hadn't been looked at by their producers for fifteen or twenty years and were already in a doubtful state. Langlois never was able to make a *qualitative* inventory, so the films just sat there. Later, in the sixties, the producers of some of these films began to remember them, because television had opened up a new market for old films, and they were aghast to find their prints weren't in mint condition. But they weren't even when they had been deposited." There was no budget for conservation, only for storage, and the Bois d'Arcy blockhouses were inadequate. If Langlois had had more money, as both Goldfayn and Martinand agree, he would have looked after these films better.

Given all the accusations of neglect against Langlois in 1968 and afterward, the testimony of S. Frederick Gronich of the MPAA is worth noting. "The fact is that we have never lost a film that we deposited with the Cinémathèque Française. This is a big statement. I repeat: the Cinémathèque never lost one of our films nor let it go bad." And through the MPAA thousands of American films were deposited with Langlois.

A part from its contributions to festivals the Cinémathèque continued to exhibit films abroad as it had done before the war. In 1953, Langlois went to Madrid to organize a homage to Marcel Carné, as well as one to René Clair which later went to London. In 1955, Langlois began a period of close cooperation with the program planners of the National Film Theatre in London, who were successively Karel Reisz, Derek Prouse, David Robinson, and, from 1959, myself.

At that time the British Film Institute was divided in two—on the one hand the archive, run by Ernest Lindgren, which was opposed both to Langlois personally and to his methods and views, and on the other the National Film Theatre, which was friendly with the Cinémathèque, thanks to James Quinn, director of the BFI, who was fond of Langlois and Mary Meerson.

Karel Reisz says that, as a program planner for the National Film Theatre, he had most of his dealings with the Cinémathèque through Mary Meerson; Reisz did not speak French very well, and in those days Langlois's English was terrible. He soon realized that it was easier to get films from Paris than from the BFI's own archive. "Ernest Lindgren," said Reisz, "only wanted to preserve films and never show them. For a season of British films I wanted a film from the twenties by a man called George Pearson. He had made some nice minor pictures. And where did we get the film? From Langlois. He had everything! He was by nature a hoarder and a collector, and he had a never-ending quest to collect films, set designs, costumes. And he wanted to show what he had. There was a rumor, you know—I have no direct evidence—that every time he came to London he would go up and down Wardour Street [where the major film offices were] and buy prints from the vault-keepers. And if you think about it, that's the most sensible way of doing it. After the general release of a film, there are always some prints left over, often in good condition, so you slip the man ten quid [about thirty dollars in those days] and there you are. . . .

"Three quarters of the films from my Stroheim season came from the Cinémathèque. Also the Buñuel season in 1955: there were many prints from Langlois, prints which he brought over personally and took back because he was afraid of having them copied. Maybe they were illegal prints. Everything I did at the National Film Theatre ended up with getting prints from the Cinémathèque—even, as I said, a lot of the British films. Once Langlois decided that you really cared about film, you could have almost anything you wanted from him.

"I must tell you one funny story about Mary Meerson. I was in Paris and Mary said, 'You English, you do not know anything about your own cinema. There's a wonderful new filmmaker in Britain now.' 'Who?' I asked. 'I don't remember his name,' she said, 'but I'll run his film for you.' And it turned out to be my own first film, *We Are the Lambeth Boys.*"

Reisz soon left the National Film Theatre and went on to become a full-time filmmaker (*Saturday Night and Sunday Morning, Morgan!, Isadora, The Gambler, The French Lieutenant's Woman*). Derek Prouse, who took his place, also confirmed that it was easier to get films from Langlois than from the National Film Archive. Langlois also got films from Prouse. The first important example was a ground-breaking program of Japanese films which Prouse organized in 1956 for the National Film Theatre. He had arranged it with the remarkable Mrs. Kawakita, film distributor and vice-president of the new film section of the Tokyo Museum of Modern Art. As Prouse remembers it, Langlois did not know Mrs. Kawakita, but he quickly made up for lost time. He came to London, saw the films, met Mrs. Kawakita, and got most of the films from her to do his own Japanese season in Paris. Thus both Paris and London discovered, among others, the films of Yasojiro Ozu.

Then there was the saga of trying to get Eisenstein's first feature film, *Strike*, from the Russians. "We were doing a Russian season," Prouse told me, "and there had been letters and cables, but all they would send me was ten minutes of *Strike*. Then, out of the blue, for the first time in the West since a screening in Berlin in 1924, a complete print arrived from Moscow. In mint condition. We showed it at the National Film Theatre, and as you remember, it was so amazing a film that there were queues round the building.

"Practically before it got onto the screen, Langlois was in London. I hadn't told him, but he had found out. Langlois always found out. I almost lost the print subsequently, because the Russians wanted a print of Hitchcock's *Blackmail* in exchange. I couldn't get it out of the National Film Archive, and the Russians began to say, 'Well, send back the print of *Strike*, then.' In desperation, I borrowed a print of *Blackmail* from the National Film Theatre, and the Russians were perfectly happy. I just couldn't let *Strike* go back to Russia, because one might never get it out again. When Langlois came over for *Strike* I got him a print, too. I just had a dupe made in some lab in Soho. I was naive at that time—I didn't know that it was something that one didn't do. I had a print, Langlois wanted a print, so it seemed natural to me that he should get one without moving heaven and earth.

A PASSION FOR FILMS

"I was never let down by Langlois, although it came pretty close sometimes. He was going to send over Fellini's first film, *Variety Lights*. The accompanying short subject was already on the screen, and there I was waiting in the Waterloo Road; the print arrived just in time to get it on the screen.

"Lindgren and Langlois were totally opposed in character and methods. Lindgren never wanted to show his films except when he was absolutely forced at gunpoint to bring one up. And he would seldom use all his budget to make prints from the originals that he refused to show. Langlois's policy was to show everything. . . . The result was that his prints were sometimes awful. Ernest's were immaculate, but they were being kept, he said, for posterity. Penelope Houston, editor of the BFI's *Sight and Sound*, once asked him, 'When does posterity begin?' "

David Robinson, Prouse's successor, first met Langlois, he says, at the big cinema exhibition that Langlois organized at the Musée National d'Art Moderne in Paris in 1955. The BFI had conceived the idea of bringing the show to London. "Later, when I became program planner at the National Film Theatre, I used to get lots of things from the Cinémathèque, but it was always a nightmare. But it was still easier than getting films from Lindgren." I asked Robinson what he thought of Karel Reisz's remark that in a hundred years' time Lindgren's methods may turn out to have been better than those Langlois employed. He didn't agree. "I remember some British distributor offered Lindgren films made by and with some famous British vaudeville artists, and Lindgren said they were all rubbish. He did finally take ten or twelve of them, but the rest were junked. So you see, Langlois's method at least gave a film the chance to survive—it may be a reduced chance, but it's a chance. If Lindgren had said, 'Okay, we'll take ten or twelve of these vaudeville films into our vaults, and throw the other three hundred into a cupboard,' well, if two hundred and fifty of them, or even two hundred and eighty had then disintegrated for lack of care, we'd still have the other fifty or the other twenty.

"Of course, the Cinémathèque's methods were peculiar and confused. But when I did the Cinémathèque tribute for the National Film Theatre in 1969, I went over to Paris, and there I gained some insight as to how the Cinémathèque actually functioned. There was Langlois in his huge bed—he was ill at the time—and he had all around him forty or so identical orange-covered exercise books, the kind schoolchildren use. There seemed to be nothing to distinguish one of these notebooks from another, but when Mary Meerson phoned and asked if the Cinémathèque had a print of *Potemkin* to send to Lille on September 8th, almost without looking, he would just grab one of those exercise books, open it, and say, 'Yes, our third print will be free then.' Then the book would vanish again."

Fortunately, I did not hear most of the cliff-hanging stories about Langlois until much later. I was soon to have my own experiences working with him, programming the National Film Theatre, but I think that if I had known ahead of time about his working habits, I might not have walked into the lion's den so blithely in the spring of 1958. In fact, although I had been once to the avenue de Messine in the early fifties (to see Dovzhenko's *Arsenal*), I can't remember having heard a word about Langlois himself until just before our first meeting. In those days Langlois kept a very low profile in connection with his public activities—and he was always even more reticent about his private life. His mother had died in 1950 and his father in 1954, but how much he grieved even his closest friends (except perhaps Mary Meerson) did not know.

□

A PASSION FOR FILMS

The year 1955 was both a terrible and a triumphant one for Langlois and the Cinémathèque. Late in 1954, he was told that the building on the avenue de Messine had been sold and that he would have to find new quarters. Langlois's first reaction was to try to arouse public opinion, and he asked François Truffaut, who was then a star journalist on the weekly magazine *Arts-Spectacles,* to write a piece protesting the threat of expulsion. Langlois still hoped that some way could be found to avoid having to move, so the tone of Truffaut's first piece reflected Langlois's attempt at a holding operation: Wouldn't it be awful if the Cinémathèque were to be thrown out of the avenue de Messine?

Help also was sought from other budding filmmakers. In the February 1955 issue of *Cahiers du Cinéma* there appeared a little note signed by Jacques Doniol-Valcroze: "We still don't know what's going to happen to the Cinémathèque. Langlois is not the kind of man to let himself be defeated, but this time it's going to be a hard struggle for him, and it's important that the whole profession and the press get behind him. For such a good cause as this, we would march on the Élysée Palace."

Langlois himself did not know what to do, and, characteristically, when faced with a threat of diminution, he reacted by an attempt at expansion. Taking advantage of the sixtieth anniversary of the first Lumière film show in Paris in 1895, he organized a huge exhibit—"60 Years of Cinema"—at the Musée National d'Art Moderne. In spite of the uncertainties which might have paralyzed the energies of another man, the show, which ran from June through September, was magnificent. I'll never forget walking into it: the entrance was dominated by two huge blowups, one of Falconetti, star of Carl Dreyer's *Passion of Joan of Arc,* and the other of Louise Brooks in a scene from Pabst's *Pandora's Box* (or *Lulu,* as it is sometimes called). When a French critic asked why he had chosen

Miss Brooks—a "nobody"—over Garbo or Dietrich, Langlois yelled, "There is no Garbo. There is no Dietrich. There is only Louise Brooks."

Thanks to the resources of the Musée d'Art Moderne, he was able to put together the first of his sumptuous catalogs. It was well illustrated and contained some of his inimitable texts, going from the prehistory of the cinema up to 1955. It was for this catalog that he wrote of Louise Brooks: "Greater than Garbo are the face, the eyes, the Joan-of-Arc-style haircut, and the smile of Louise Brooks. Those who have seen her can never forget her."

The huge space given him by the museum was filled by objects, photographs, costumes, and set designs. And in a small screening room one could see films; there I finally managed to catch up with Chaplin's *The Circus*, which at that time could not be seen anywhere else in the world.

So this exhibition, with its screening room, was a temporary solution to the loss of the avenue de Messine building, for in spite of the articles by Truffaut and Doniol-Valcroze, it was lost. The threatened march on the Élysée Palace, however, did not have to take place. Help came from an unexpected quarter: M. Louis Cross, director of the Musée Pédagogique. He had been one of those who had faithfully attended the screenings at the avenue de Messine, and his museum on the rue d'Ulm contained a theater. Not only was it a larger room than the Cinémathèque's, it was also situated on the Left Bank, in the Latin Quarter, and this was to bring a whole new audience.

Paris is, relatively speaking, a small city, but the avenue de Messine was in an upper-middle-class residential area, and dead at night. There were no cafés, it was not close to a metro station, and it was in a part of Paris where no one would think of going unless he or she lived there. The rue d'Ulm, on the other hand, is a narrow street running downhill from the Panthéon southward. It, too, is deserted at night, but it is only a few hundred yards from the bustling boulevard St. Michel with its enormous student population, many of whom welcomed the chance of seeing good films cheaply. Langlois took over the theater, and it was an enormous success, thanks in part to another Truffaut article telling everyone where the new cinema was and how to get there.

Although the main advantage of the new theater (apart from its situation) was the fact that it had about 250 seats (compared with the 50 at the avenue de Messine), there were nights when one raced round the corner of the Panthéon to look down the rue d'Ulm to seey if the line for tickets had extended upstairs (the theater was in the basement) and wound its way out onto the street. That was a bad sign: if the queue had reached the street, there wasn't much chance of getting in. And although as at the avenue de Messine there were sometimes performances with only a dozen people in the hall, there were others when the line went four blocks up to the Panthéon itself. In those cases, they were lining up for tickets to the *following* screening.

But the problem of office space was still not solved. For a short period, the staff was all in one room in the avenue de l'Opéra, then in producer Sacha Gordine's sumptuous apartment in the rue Spontini. Only in 1957 were they able to find suitable space, a four-story building in the rue de Courcelles. It had been a luxurious private residence, and the layout was formal. In those days there was even a doorkeeper to screen visitors.

It was he who, on a Saturday afternoon in July 1960, ran into Mary Meerson's office, saying, "There's two men here who want to see Henri Langlois, and one of them says he's Buster Keaton. But he can't fool me: he must be a crank. Shall I call the police or just throw them out?"

Crossing the Seine

Mary Meerson rushed into the lobby shouting, "Buster, Buster!" She ran over to him, grabbed him, and picked him off the floor. Keaton was of course astonished. But he kept his great stone face. They went up to see Langlois, sat down and discussed which prints Keaton and his agent, Raymond Rohauer, had. For Langlois, although he was less effusive than Mary, it was one of the greatest days of his life: Buster Keaton walking into the Cinémathèque on a quiet summer Saturday afternoon. But he found time to make a phone call, and when they all went downstairs, there was a cameraman who filmed the four of them inside the Cinémathèque and outside in the Parc Monceau nearby.

It was on that day that the idea was first discussed of a tribute to Keaton, to take place at the rue d'Ulm. The real planning took place the following year: Rohauer and Langlois pooled their prints to make the most complete retrospective of Keaton's films ever shown. Keaton, although extremely shy, was persuaded by Rohauer to go to Paris in February 1962.

On the night of the opening, when Keaton and Rohauer approached the rue d'Ulm theater, the line went all the way up the hill. There were so many people inside that Keaton was almost crushed by the crowd. He was glad when it was over. "Where did all those people come from?" he wondered. There were celebrities, of course, like Abel Gance, but what surprised him most was the large number of young people. How, he wondered, had they heard of him? He didn't realize that Langlois had been showing some Keaton films for years.

The rue d'Ulm period was for many the Golden Age of the Cinémathèque. Truffaut (who says that he has forgotten a lot of what happened at the avenue de Messine) particularly remembers the Ingmar Bergman retrospective in 1957, the year before he shot *The 400 Blows*. "There was a fantastic atmosphere about that retrospective. We had all seen *Summer with*

A PASSION FOR FILMS

Monika, and then at Cannes we saw *Smiles of a Summer Night.* Then Langlois brought all the Bergman films from Sweden— without subtitles, of course. For two weeks, we came to the rue d'Ulm every night. There was this Swedish girl who trans- lated for us."

"That's odd," I said. "Langlois always said that the fact that he showed films without subtitles was what taught you all mise-en-scène, because, not understanding what was being said, you really had to concentrate on how the films were put together."

"Yes," replied Truffaut, "but the Bergman films were dia- logue films—you really had to understand what was being said. It is true, though, that one can learn a lot about cinema if you see foreign films without subtitles. When I see films in America, I don't understand a word of the dialogue—I just look at the images. I can tell you more about the lighting and the shots of film I saw in America than about any French film."

One more contradiction then: one needs translation for Bergman films but not for American ones. But perhaps the contradiction is only apparent. One could argue that Ameri- can films are easier to follow—without any knowledge of En- glish—than Bergman films. Then, too, most French film- makers understand more English than they will admit or even than they are aware of.

The first year on the rue d'Ulm was a wonderful one. Lan- glois started off with three great shows—"60 Years of German Cinema," "60 Years of Scandinavian Cinema," and "60 Years of British Cinema"—and a homage to Méliès. Although problems with FIAF were brewing, the British show was pre- sented with the cooperation of the British Film Institute, and the Scandinavian show (more properly, the Danish/Swedish show) had the cooperation of the Swedish and Danish film archives. The year ended with a monster show called "75 Years of Cinema." A mimeographed program listed all the screenings scheduled for the period from October 1956 through June 1957—and this was almost the last time the Cinémathèque was able to publish a program so far in advance. (Of course, the film announced was not necessarily the film shown, but still . . .) The pretext for the program was the twentieth anniversary of the Cinémathèque, and although individual films were shown as such, it consisted mainly of a series of homages: Vigo, Buñuel, Robert Aldrich—whom Langlois had already recognized as living proof that an "author" could still exist in Hollywood—Brecht, von Stroheim, Rossellini,* Dovzhenko, Joris Ivens, Maurice Tourneur (only one film, however), Visconti, Jiří Trnka (the Czech puppet-filmmaker), Lumière, Kurosawa, Cavalcanti, E. A. Dupont (*Variety*), Helmut Käutner, Franju, Germaine Dulac, Sjöström, and René Clair.

An unexceptional list, with the exception of Aldrich and perhaps Käutner. But there were other important "homages" in this series: one to the producer Léon Gaumont, one to producer Charles Pathé, and one to producers Jesse Lasky and Adolph Zukor (Paramount). Long before *Cahiers du Cinéma* admitted that producers had their importance, Langlois was spotlighting their role. As Bernard Martinand, one of Langlois's best programmers, put it to me: "Langlois was the first archivist to understand the reality of film production—and he was fascinated by the great producers. When he said later that

---

*Langlois was one of the first to realize that Rossellini's career had not stopped with *Open City* and *Paisan*. In 1956, he understood that *Flowers of St. Francis* marked a new and important development in Rossellini's career, and he was among the first to acclaim his films with Ingrid Bergman—*Journey to Italy* (also called *Strangers*), *Europa 51* (*The Greatest Love*), and *Fear* (*Angst/La Paura*).

A PASSION FOR FILMS

the cinema was created by illiterate fur traders, he did not mean this disparagingly. He thought that it was precisely because these pioneers were illiterate—i.e., uncultured—that they were able more quickly to grasp the importance and the significance of the cinema." And Langlois praised Léon Gaumont, who, he pointed out, was by tradition and education at the level of the average Frenchman, but who nonetheless allowed Marcel L'Herbier to make *Rose France*; even when *Rose France* was a box-office failure, Gaumont persevered, and in spite of the fun poked at him by the "professionals" (including, alas, Feuillade), he went on to produce L'Herbier's *Eldorado*, *Villa Destin*, and *Don Juan et Faust*.

Charles Pathé, who like Adolph Zukor actually *was* in the fur business before starting a traveling cinema, created the world's first cinema empire. Nevertheless, as Langlois wrote, "If Abel Gance was able to make *La Roue* and *J'Accuse!*, and if those works were able to be shown without being cut or disfigured, it was thanks to Pathé, who always upheld Gance's right to make films as he saw fit."[3]

Langlois was so even-handed that he could appreciate how much Stroheim suffered at the hands of his producers and yet praise Lasky and Zukor for their roles as pioneers of the American cinema, and he added, "It would be absurd, antihistorical, and untrue to dissociate Griffith and Ince from Zukor and Lasky."[4] In this homage (which coincided with the thirty-fifth anniversary of French Paramount) Langlois also pointed out the links between France and Paramount: Louis Mercanton's *Queen Elizabeth* with Sarah Bernhardt was Paramount's first success. And during World War I several French directors—most notably Maurice Tourneur—played an essential role in the elaboration of the "Paramount style" long before Lubitsch arrived from Germany. Later, Langlois observed, the current was reversed when Paramount loaned Gloria Swanson to France for Perret's *Madame Sans-Gêne*, and it was thanks to French Paramount that Cavalcanti, Marcel Achard, and Henri Jeanson were able to make their first talkies in France—at the very moment when Maurice Chevalier was triumphing on the sound stages of Paramount in Hollywood.

Another triumph at the rue d'Ulm was the Louise Brooks retrospective in 1958. We have seen how much Langlois admired Miss Brooks; somehow, Langlois had discovered that she was living in New York. As Miss Brooks told me, "It was Langlois who rediscovered me. I was living in New York on First Avenue, and one day a man in a trench coat came to see me. It was Jim Card [curator of the Eastman House film collection in Rochester]. He had just come from Paris, where Langlois had shown him the two films I made with Pabst. When Card told me what Langlois was saying about me, I thought, 'He must be kidding!' This was the first time I had heard anything about myself in thirty years."

In 1958 Louise Brooks went to Paris for a retrospective of her films on the rue d'Ulm. But she spent most of her time in Paris in bed. "I loved that hotel they put me up at—the Royal Monçeau. It was near that wonderful building with those marble pillars and the red damask where the Cinémathèque had its offices [rue de Courcelles]. But I mostly stayed in bed and read. Lotte would come to see me every day. She always kept talking about that German director she admired so much—you know, the one that made *Sunrise*. As for Henri, well, I didn't understand a word he said. In those days his English wasn't very good, and even though I had lived for a while in Paris when I was making *Prix de Beauté* [1930], my French was no good. So I talked to Lotte, to Mrs. Kawakita, and to some Americans [Elliott Stein and Kenneth Anger]. I got up once for the big reception.

"Oh, yes, I did go to that wonderful apartment where Henri and Mary lived together. I adored Mary's sister Hélène. I got on better with her than I did with Mary or Henri. . . . There was always this mystery about Hélène. One day I asked Henri, 'Who are Mary and Hélène?' And all he said was, 'They're gypsies, gypsies . . .' I didn't know what he meant by that."

As it turned out, the Paris tribute was the first of a series; Miss Brooks went to Copenhagen and even back to the scene of her first triumph, Berlin. Of course the great mystery is not that Louise Brooks was rediscovered but how she was ever forgotten. When she said that she had never heard or read a word about herself for thirty years, I asked her whether she wasn't exaggerating a bit. "No, no," she cried. "Don't forget, we made *Pandora's Box* in the summer of 1928. Talkies were coming in. I know that when the film came out in New York it was released at the Fifty-fifth Street Playhouse and no one saw it.* And *Diary of a Lost Girl* . . . that was Pabst's last silent film. If you look at it closely, it falls apart towards the end. That was because he was so eager to get it finished in order to start on *Westfront,* his first talkie."

So the films, like Miss Brooks, fell into that black hole left by the arrival of the talking film: no longer of any commercial value, they disappeared from the world's screens. Miss Brooks herself says that she does not get much pleasure out of seeing her old films. She claims never to have seen *A Girl in Every Port,* even though she adored Howard Hawks. ("He was my dream director.") And when Card showed *Pandora's Box* to her, she didn't really see it: "I talked all the way through it.

New York Times review, December 2, 1929 (Mordaunt Hall): "Miss Brooks is attractive and she moves her head and eyes at the proper moment, but whether she is endeavoring to express joy, woe, anger or satisfaction it is often difficult to decide."

Crossing the Seine

You see, I don't like seeing my films. I wasn't an actress like Garbo, who was always *doing* something you could watch; with me, there's nothing for me to look at. I wasn't really doing anything . . . it was all unconscious."

As anyone who has ever seen *Pandora's Box* or *A Girl in Every Port* knows, Miss Brooks's performances are among the greatest in cinema, and thanks to Langlois and the other archivists, the rest of us can still see them.

7

Friends and Enemies

I first met Langlois in 1958. The editor of *Sight and Sound* was starting a series of monographs on film directors, and she asked me to do one on Max Ophüls. But there were many of his films of the thirties that I hadn't seen. "No problem," said Penelope Houston, editor of the magazine. "I'll arrange all that with the Cinémathèque." But she arranged it with Mary Meerson, not Langlois.

I went to the rue de Courcelles offices and told the door-keeper that I had an appointment with Mary Meerson. "Wait," I was told. I went into the lobby and waited, from ten in the morning until one. Then a mysterious messenger appeared to tell me I had better go out to lunch, because Mme. Meerson wasn't ready to receive me yet. I was surprised and a little discouraged but decided I had better follow instructions.

When I got back, I was graduated from the lobby of the building to an empty office, where I sat for another hour. By this time, I was not only discouraged, I was bored, and as there was a typewriter in the office, I decided to catch up on my correspondence.

Suddenly, a wild-eyed man, enormous and disheveled, erupted into the room and asked me what the hell I thought I was doing there. I said bravely who I was, that I was waiting for a Mme. Meerson, and that I had been sent by *Sight and Sound*—the magazine of the British Film Institute—to see some Max Ophüls films.

That did it. "How dare you come from the BFI and use our typewriters, you who duped my print of *L'Age d'Or* and sent it to Haifa?" I had heard that someone at the BFI had indeed duplicated Buñuel's film and sent prints all over the world, but I had had nothing to do with it. I tried to explain to Langlois that I wasn't British, that I wasn't even on the BFI payroll, that I had been hired just to do this one little job, that I had come all the way from London—and when could I start seeing the films, please.

At that point an equally huge woman came into the room—no doubt she had heard the screaming—and began to yell at Langlois, asking him how dare he insult *her* guest. That was Mary Meerson. Then the two of them began to scream at each other. I didn't know what to do; it was a terrifying situation. Here I was, on my first assignment, and determined to see those films, which could not be seen anywhere else in the world.

Eventually, tired of arguing with her, Langlois turned back to me and asked what the hell I thought I was doing using their typewriter. This was where I had come in, so to speak, but I stood my ground, more out of the shame of going back to London empty-handed than out of bravery. Then either because he had not succeeded in frightening me away, or because he understood that I really wanted to see the Ophüls films, he calmed down, gave me a half smile, almost winked—as if to signify that I had passed the test—and said, "Okay, Madame Meerson will arrange your screenings."

So she did, and so began a professional relationship and a personal friendship which were to last almost twenty years. In a way, that first meeting summed it all up. Langlois was not an easy person to deal with. He was paranoid; he was bigger than life, not only physically but emotionally. But he had the films I wanted to see, and he did show them to me. The Ophüls films I had come to see had not been preserved by anyone else, because, after *Liebelei*, Ophüls was thought to have dropped to the level of a commercial filmmaker. But Langlois, before Bazin, before Truffaut, before Andrew Sarris, was an auteurist.

It is true that most of Ophüls's films of the thirties were not great—with the dazzling exception of his Italian film *La Signora di Tutti*—but it is also true that seeing them is essential to an understanding of the path Ophüls followed from *Liebelei* to the last great quartet: *La Ronde, Le Plaisir, The Earrings of Madame de . . .* , and *Lola Montès*.

Because of my "success" with the dreaded Langlois—back in London I found that almost everybody at the BFI had been sure he wouldn't show me anything—the BFI asked me to mount a huge French season the following year at the National Film Theatre, covering the period from 1929 to 1959. Langlois and I had to work out the program together. Everyone said he was impossibly dictatorial, but I did not find this to be true. At least not with the features: he insisted on our showing a few rather odd shorts, made by favorites of his, but that presented no great problem. The only serious discussion I remember was about Grémillon's *Gueule d'Amour*, a 1937 film I had seen in a revival house in Paris and liked. "But that's one of the commercial films he was obliged to make in the late thirties," said Langlois. "You can't show that." I held out, saying it may have been commercial, but it was also damned good, and that it had one of Jean Gabin's best performances. Finally he gave in, with a groan and sneer at my "English" taste. I was pleased to discover that The Cinémathèque began to screen *Gueule d'Amour* regularly a few years later.

On the opening night, when Langlois was to be introduced from the stage of the NFT, he, James Quinn, and I were sitting in the club room; suddenly Langlois asked if anyone had any black shoe polish. I was surprised, because Langlois never bothered about his shoes; but the assistant manager found some polish. Whereupon Langlois crossed his legs and began applying it to his ankle—to camouflage a rather large hole in his sock.

The season was successful; David Thomson wrote: "In June 1960, in the third part of a season of French films, the London National Film Theatre showed the best version available of *Lola Montès*. The season itself . . . is one for which I and some others will always be grateful. Above all, it had placed Renoir in his rightful eminence. But it had introduced me to several other major figures, and because it coincided with the incoming tide of the New Wave it served to stress the abiding themes and vitality of the French cinema."[1]

Langlois had come to London several times during the course of the preparation of the French season, but he spent most of his time there drawing up a kind of contract between the British Film Institute and the Cinémathèque. He had composed a complicated letter of agreement, which I had to translate. I didn't understand at the time why Langlois attached so much importance to it: later I realized that he must have been preparing for a break with FIAF, which by then had spread round the world, with member archives on six continents. He wanted to make sure that the relationship he had with the British Film Institute would survive.

L anglois's departure from FIAF was a momentous event in the rather recondite story of that organization and its internal battles and power struggles. Did he leave or was he pushed out? The answer is difficult to ascertain. Even harder to determine are the reasons why he would want to leave or why they would want him to go. The several versions of the story contradict each other and are difficult to verify or to reconcile.

One version was given to me by someone outside FIAF, S. Frederick Gronich. According to him, some members of FIAF were indulging in practices that were either illegal or unethical. If Langlois had remained within FIAF, sooner or later their actions would reflect on him. Langlois had the complete trust of directors like Chaplin and Alfred Hitchcock who had given him their films. When Chaplin, for example, wanted to store all his nitrate prints and negatives with the Cinémathèque, Langlois said, "Yes, but on one condition. I'll give you a whole bunker, you put your films in it, you put *your* lock on it, and you take *your* key with you." There were so many Chaplin films floating around the archive world that Langlois wouldn't run the risk of Chaplin's even suspecting that they had come from him.

"There were other reasons, however," said Gronich.

Friends and Enemies

"Langlois had more than his share of artistic temperament and did not brook disagreement gracefully. Then, too, he was well placed to acquire films, especially American films, because the European and Middle Eastern divisions of the MPAA's member companies were then based in Paris, and they favored Langlois, so when they had finished with, say, the Swedish subtitled print of an American film, they would bring the print back from Sweden and give it to Langlois. This was all right with the countries that didn't have their own archive, but any country that did was naturally annoyed that a print subtitled in its language would be given to Langlois rather than to its own archive. This caused dissension, and we tried to cool it by encouraging the major companies to deposit some unwanted prints with the Cinémathèque Française and some with the local archives. In those days films went into release with a larger number of prints than now— five or ten then, even in the smaller countries, whereas now you release only one or two prints. But the basic problem was the ethics of the acquisition policies of the other archives— which in their early days probably were no worse than Langlois had been in the thirties, doing the best he could to get prints. But something had changed in the meanwhile: television had increased the value of old films, and more and more pirated prints began floating around.

"At that point we became very conscious of the duplicating activities of some of the other archives. I don't want to be quoted on individual archives. But I could name six or seven western European ones that would borrow a print from another country and then dupe it. They weren't 'misusing' the prints, because they weren't commercializing them; but they were showing a lack of respect for the copyright owners.

"Furthermore, they wanted to acquire *permanent* control and possession of such prints, whereas Langlois and I, to

A PASSION FOR FILMS

avoid anyone, particularly governments, laying hands on what we had, worked out together the concept of the extended loan deposit. For example, with Metro we worked out what I thought to be the ideal formula: they would rent him a print of theirs for one franc a year; thus, it remained their property, legally."

Behind what Gronich told me lay a fundamental difference between Langlois and many FIAF archivists. Langlois always believed in respecting the rights of the owners of the films, whereas many other archivists hold the view, which they have expressed openly, that they couldn't care less about the capitalist system of ownership. As far as they are concerned, the great films belong to the world and should be shown to whoever wants to see them. Some archivists went even further: according to Gronich, Raymond Borde at a UNESCO meeting (where he was acting as adviser to an archivist from East Germany) tried to promulgate the theory that if a film is screened in a country, it automatically becomes part of its cultural heritage . . . and therefore should not thereafter be removed from that country.

Langlois objected that a rights holder like Chaplin would never have had enough money to produce his later work—*A King in New York, The Countess from Hong Kong*—if he hadn't held on to the rights to his films, judiciously re-releasing them from time to time and financing his later films with money they earned.

Another version of the break with FIAF was given to me by Freddy Buache, head of the Cinémathèque Suisse. A great friend of Langlois, he is also a friend of Raymond Borde (Cinémathèque de Toulouse), one of Langlois's detractors.

"His leaving FIAF," says Buache, "was more in the nature of a caprice. He had always liked to run things at FIAF—organize in the back-room way so that he could get what he

Friends and Enemies

wanted. His principle was to divide and conquer. And one must say that at that period, FIAF had swelled its ranks to include men of a different stripe from the founders and early members. * FIAF has evolved a lot over the years, especially since the departure of Henri. Today FIAF is no longer made up of 'film lovers' but rather film technicians. I don't mean this derogatorily, but there is a difference. And that 1960 Congress was precisely the turning point in the history of FIAF. Langlois had the impression FIAF was getting too bureaucratic and was spending more time discussing rules and procedure than in exchanging films. And at that moment, Ledoux of the Belgian Cinémathèque had achieved a certain position in FIAF, and Langlois decided that if that was the way things were going, he would continue alone—outside FIAF. And when he walked out of the meeting, I followed him because I was *organically* linked to the Cinémathèque Française. But I don't think one will ever be able to define precisely why Langlois split from FIAF.

"Henri was always haunted by the notion of illegal duping. And I must say he used his collection of unique films to gain power. But Ledoux slowly became more and more important at FIAF meetings, and became the man who wanted to take over FIAF from Langlois. I know there are—were—a number of *cinémathèques* which trafficked in illegal prints, but I don't

---

*From the original four founding members, FIAF had grown to include over thirty member archives. Some of the more important film-producing countries had three archives (Milan, Rome, and Turin in Italy), and there were two archives in a country as small as Uruguay. Other nations represented in FIAF included Argentina, Australia, Austria, Brazil, Bulgaria, Canada, China, Colombia, Czechoslovakia, Denmark, Egypt, Finland, East and West Germany, Hungary, Iran, Japan, Morocco, The Netherlands, Norway, Peru, Poland, Portugal, Spain, and Yugoslavia.

think Belgium was one of them: Ledoux respected copyrights. On the other hand, things can happen against one's will. I had trouble myself with a film lent to some people who I thought were honest and who turned out not to be, and as it happened, it was a Chaplin film, too. It's also true that the eastern European *cinémathèques* used to circulate pirated prints of Chaplin's *Woman of Paris*, which they would offer us in exchange for something they wanted. But I don't think that problems like these were really the cause of the split.

"What I do remember is that from the very beginning of the congress there was an animosity between Ledoux and Langlois, and then Langlois gathered all his papers together and with a gesture said, 'Under these conditions, I'm leaving FIAF.' Some of us followed him: me, Mrs. Kawakita of Tokyo, James Card of Eastman House, Rochester. We walked out, thinking, 'Henri is right.' But I don't think it was about anything very precise. It is true, too, and that was just like him, that he had threatened to walk out previously, and I'm sure that in 1960 he expected the others to come after him to bring him back."

But they didn't. The secretary of FIAF, Marion Michelle, felt that FIAF was not sufficiently independent of the Cinémathèque. Ms. Michelle claimed with some justification that she didn't have direct access to FIAF correspondence, that letters were kept from her. So when the executive committee met after the Stockholm Congress, they took a vote of no confidence in Langlois.

"However," continued Buache, "the break with FIAF didn't really cause him any trouble. He and the prestige of the Cinémathèque were so great that all the other archives concluded bilateral agreements with him for exchanging films. It was much more dangerous for people like me: the Swiss Cinémathèque was cut off from all FIAF members, and I had only

Friends and Enemies

Langlois to depend on—and he could be difficult, you know. I was isolated, he wasn't. Especially with the eastern European countries; the prestige of Paris was so great in their eyes that they all continued to send him films. But not to me: when I asked the Russians to lend me films, they said, 'No, you're not a FIAF member; we can only resume relations with you when you come back to FIAF,' while at the same time they were sending films to Langlois.

"But finally, I had to explain to Langlois that I was not in the same position as James Card or Mrs. Kawakita or himself. I was all alone in Switzerland, and everybody, including Ledoux, refused to deal with me. I said to Langlois, 'I've got to have relations with the other archives. I'm not in your position; no one is interested in Lausanne. I've got to return to FIAF.' And he said, 'Go back—no problem.' Furthermore, he was sufficiently Machiavellian to realize that if I went back to FIAF, I could be a convenient go-between. *

"Raymond Borde was a personal friend of mine, and I saw him start the Toulouse Cinémathèque in the fifties. I went there, saw Borde and Étienne Chaumeton (who together wrote the first book defining and celebrating the American *film noir*), and put them in contact with Langlois. But from then on, it's difficult for me to speak about their relations, because Langlois and Borde each accused the other of having stolen his films. Each of them had deposited films with the other and apparently hadn't returned them.

"Borde began by having considerable esteem for Langlois. I remember the days when Borde would do anything for Langlois or Mary Meerson. He was totally devoted to the Cinémathèque Française. But then, when he began to feel that he

---

* And indeed I remember Langlois saying about the 1961 Congress, "I'll shine by my absence—and my spies!" [—R. R.]

had acquired a certain authority, that he could replace the Cinémathèque Française in FIAF as the French member, he became extremely nasty. There was hatred, but in my opinion it was really a love-hate relationship. I always thought there was a grand passion there. However, I think Borde's manner of expressing his hatred for Langlois was extremely indelicate. But that's passion for you.

"To come back to the congress, I think that Langlois felt threatened by Ledoux, who wanted to organize FIAF differently, and simply chose a pretext—which I can't remember— to say 'I'm leaving,' with the hope that they wouldn't let him go. Ledoux believed in a tighter organization—during the Langlois period there was *no* organization; everything ran on pure emotion. Ledoux began to raise the problems of cataloging, methods of conservation, catalogs, things that Langlois couldn't have cared less about, and certainly not in Ledoux's somewhat technocratic way. In any case, Langlois's departure marked the turning point in FIAF—it was no longer a group of film fanatics.

"But however much I loved him, Langlois was impossible at times. He was like a spoiled child, continually indulging in caprices. FIAF wanted to become a respectable international organization, and that annoyed him very much. They wanted to deposit the statutes of FIAF with the French government— which Langlois had never done. They wanted the organization to become more disciplined.

"If I had it to do all over again? Yes, I'd still have left with Langlois. I owed everything to him, and I think in some ways he was right to want to keep FIAF as a group of friends rather than let it become a technocratic organization. I didn't go back to FIAF until 1972."

With the departure of Langlois, all the original founders of FIAF were gone. Olwen Vaughan had left the British Film Institute during the war; Frank Hensel had returned to private

life. Iris Barry was named lifetime honorary president, but she had retired from the Museum of Modern Art in 1951. She thought she was suffering from incurable cancer, and she went back to Europe, as she thought, to die. But fate was kinder than she expected. She lived until 1969, in the town of Fayence in southern France.

I saw her occasionally during those last years. One night I had dinner in London with her, Joseph Losey, and Losey's wife, Patricia. As the dinner wore on, Iris became maudlin. "I betrayed Henri," she said "and he was my friend. But I had to betray him, because FIAF was more important." As she herself was not at the Stockholm Congress, I was never sure what she meant by her "betrayal," but she obviously felt strongly about it.

Langlois, Margareta Akermark told me, wanted to raise a monument over her grave in Fayence. He never got around to doing it, but at least he tried. There is no worthy monument to Iris Barry in the Museum of Modern Art. Ms. Akermark, who attempted to persuade the powers-that-be to name the film department's study center after Miss Barry, was told that things get named for people only if they have contributed money to the museum. The fact that Miss Barry had contributed so much of her life was considered irrelevant.

With the end of the Cinémathèque's connection with FIAF, a new era began in Paris, perhaps the most brilliant seven years of the Cinémathèque's history.

My happiest and most rewarding times with Langlois were at restaurants. Talking in his office was difficult: the phone would never stop ringing; there was always some crisis. So I learned that the best way of seeing Langlois whenever I came to Paris was to meet him for lunch.

In the early sixties, we invariably went to a restaurant near

the Courcelles offices called Le Vigny. It was a pleasant place, and they were always happy to see Langlois. But there was a ritual: we couldn't go there without first stopping to buy the early edition of *France-Soir*. Langlois, a Scorpio, had to read the daily astrology column. I don't know how completely he believed in it, because although he usually would look up from the paper and crow, "You see, I knew I was right; there *is* a spy at the Cinémathèque," sometimes he would put the paper down sadly and say, "You know, she's losing her grip, that columnist. She hasn't got anything right today." I think that Langlois used astrology simply to confirm things he already knew or thought he knew. Whether or not one "believes" in astrological predictions, one can recognize astrological types. Langlois certainly corresponded to the usual descriptions: with an instinctive, imperious nature, volcanic, the Scorpio is essentially a ferocious individualist, rebellious, capable of flying into a rage, irritable, violent.

Once he had decided he liked you, everything changed. He may have harbored suspicions, but by and large, if he accepted you, he was both loyal and generous. And food did calm him. As one can imagine from his size, he ate a lot. But even though in another person obesity like his might have been unpleasant or repulsive, such was the excitement of Langlois's conversation that one simply did not think about how fat he was.

Many theories have been advanced as to why Langlois, formerly so thin, had gradually become fat. W. H. Auden has provided one possible explanation: "I would say that fatness in the male is the physical expression of a psychological wish to withdraw from sexual competition, and, by combining mother and child in his own person, to become emotionally self-sufficient. The Greeks thought of Narcissus as a slender youth, but I think they were wrong. I see him as a middle-

aged man with a corporation, for, however ashamed he may be of displaying it in public, in private a man with a belly loves it dearly; it may be an unprepossessing child to look at, but he has borne it all by himself."[2] On the other hand, Godfrey Smith, who used this quote from Auden in the *Sunday Times* (London), April 6, 1980, said that it may be that a certain kind of fat man has, by choosing obesity, deliberately preselected his own death. Some psychologists, however, prefer to think of obesity as being caused by a kind of "alimentary orgasm": food takes the place of sex.

Over lunch, his first question was, "Have you any gossips for me?" I don't know what he was like before the FIAF troubles, but afterward, he always wanted to hear what was new at the British Film Institute, and particularly what Ernest Lindgren, his archenemy, was doing—or, more important, not doing. These tidbits were so important for Langlois that I used to prepare a short list in my head before meeting him, because he would be disappointed if I said, "Oh well, everything's much the same."

The purpose of my visits to Paris was usually to ask Langlois for films for a program at the National Film Theatre. But such questions would have to wait until the main course was finished and dessert ordered. It didn't always go smoothly. After he had agreed to help me do a given season, and had worked out in his mental instant retrieval system where the prints were, he became impatient if I tried to pin him down as to when the prints would be sent or how (diplomatic pouch, air shipment, or occasionally sleeping car, thus avoiding, in most cases, the problem of import/export licenses and customs). Although (or maybe because) he knew perfectly well I was American, whenever he wanted to get a dig at me, he would always start with "You English are so . . ." whatever. And of course it is true that the National Film Theatre was not run

A PASSION FOR FILMS

like the Cinémathèque. We had *not* trained our audiences to be surprised if the film announced was the film actually shown. We sent out booklets four or six weeks in advance describing the films, giving the dates, with a booking form for advanced reservations. Langlois refused to take this into account. In Paris, after all, the films were announced only a week at a time, and his audience had been trained to expect anything. The only way I could get him to cooperate was to say, little-boy-like, "It's not *my* fault; I have to work for them, and I have to do things their way." That would bring out his latent paternal instincts, and half contemptuously but half reassuringly, he would say, "Don't worry, you'll get the films on time." And we did get them—just on time, usually, but nonetheless on time.

If the luncheon ritual never changed, the restaurants did. I remember automatically heading toward the Vigny one day, only to be told by Langlois, "Oh, we don't go there any more; the restaurant's gone down. Now we go to the Courcelles." It didn't seem like an improvement to me, and later Kenneth Anger explained to me why Langlois changed restaurants every nine months or so. He never paid on the spot, but charged it to his account; when the bill finally came in, Langlois never had enough money to pay it. The odd thing is that although he eventually paid up, he never went back to the restaurant to which he had owed money. Irrationally, he resented the fact that the bills were so high, or that he had been obliged to scrounge around to pay for meals he had *already* eaten.

He usually walked around without money, as a matter of fact: only if he and I were going somewhere special (where he had no account) would Mary stuff a couple of hundred-franc notes into his breast pocket on the way out of the building. (She would almost never come with us: either she wanted to

Friends and Enemies

leave us alone, or she wanted to be alone in the Cinémathèque without Henri.)

In 1961, a year after the big French season, I arranged a
Visconti retrospective in London in the autumn. Most of the
prints came from local sources, but I had a problem with
Senso, because the only print in Britain was the cut, dubbed
version called *The Wanton Countess*. Henri came to the rescue. He said, "We'll fix it all up at the Venice Film Festival
with Comencini and the Milan Cinémathèque." And we did
fix it up: to simplify matters for Comencini it was arranged
that on my way back to London from Venice I would stay
awake until I got to Milan—actually, not even the Central
Station, because late at night the Simplon-Orient Express
would stop at a suburban station. There at Milano-Lambrate I
was to look out the window and be ready to take the cans of
film into my sleeping compartment. It seemed to me a highly
dubious undertaking: I wasn't sure the print would be there,
or that the man carrying it would have enough time to find
me while the train made its brief stop. But sure enough, we
pulled into the station, I opened the window, and saw on the
deserted platform a man with ten cans of film. He hoisted
them up to me, I stowed them in the luggage rack, and that's
how an original print of *Senso* got to London.

By 1962 we had already gone through two more restaurants
and had graduated to La Savoie, a rather better restaurant
than the ones we had frequented. It was there that we organized three of the biggest programs I ever did for London:
first, a retrospective of the films of Fritz Lang; second, a complete Jean Renoir show; and finally, a more esoteric but fascinating program called "Dovzhenko and Soviet Cinema of the
30's." Once again, Langlois's belief in collecting as much as
possible proved to be invaluable. One of Dovzhenko's early
sound films was called *Ivan* (not to be confused with *Ivan the*

A PASSION FOR FILMS

Terrible or *The Childhood of Ivan*). According to the books, it was not successful, but Langlois had got it from the Russians anyhow. And it proved to be a revelation. One could see why people had not liked it at the time—it had plot and structural weaknesses—but it was extremely beautiful. And thanks to Langlois, we (I did the season with the late Robert Vas) did discover some little-known gems from the 1930s—a period in Russian film history that was not highly thought of.

Arranging the Renoir show was the most fun, however, because we had to deal with the legendary Madame Doinel,* who looked after Renoir's interests and films in France and who lived in his house on the avenue Frochot. Never has an artist's house and street seemed more suitable than did the avenue Frochot for Renoir. A "private street," it curled its way in a semicircle up a hill, where it stopped short in a dead end just behind the "nudie" shows of the place Pigalle. When you were in the little "street," you seemed miles from Paris in some peaceful provincial town.

Of course, Langlois was not only helping me to program; apart from running the theater on the rue d'Ulm, he was arranging retrospective shows for other film libraries and for the Cannes and Venice festivals. In 1962 he had shown a small number of unknown early Mizoguchi films at Cannes; for many critics, they were the highlight of the festival.

Langlois also found time to help me do one of my favorite NFT seasons, which I called "School of Vienna." The idea was that although Austrian films had never been particularly distinguished, an amazing number of great film directors had been born and brought up in Vienna—Stroheim, Lang,

---

*Truffaut "adapted" her last name for the character played by Jean-Pierre Léaud in the "Antoine Doinel" films: *The 400 Blows, Stolen Kisses*, etc.

Pabst, and Sternberg, for example—and that furthermore, however individual their talents, all of them shared a common world view: a cynicism born perhaps of the experience of the dying Austro-Hungarian Empire, a fascination for the baroque, the decadent, and at the same time, especially in the cases of Sternberg and Stroheim, a slightly perverse sense of eroticism. Most of the prints were to come from the Cinémathèque, and I was particularly pleased to be able to get the sound-synchronized version of *The Wedding March*, which had never been shown in Britain.

He didn't always approve of the films I wanted to borrow, but after a few slighting references to my "English" taste, he would agree to let me have them. And he was constantly suggesting films and showing them to me. These screenings didn't always take place on the day planned, and I remember that in the case of the Soviet season Robert Vas and I spent four fruitless days in Paris waiting for the screenings to start. Vas became discouraged and said we ought to go back to London: we were never going to see anything. "Don't despair," I said, "you'll see." And sure enough, we did get to view everything—but in a two-day marathon, from ten in the morning to nine at night. It would have been so much easier for us and cheaper for Langlois—no overtime for the projectionists—to have spread the screenings over the week, but he just didn't work that way. Like some journalists, he could function only with a deadline hanging over his head. Then the adrenaline would begin to flow, he would get on the phone, and the whole thing would be taken care of.

In the same way, he hardly ever answered letters. First of all, he didn't like to leave written traces that "could be used against him." He also had the Italian attitude: if it's really important, they'll send a telegram or phone. Another reason for his reluctance to write letters was that although he dictated

them to his secretary, he insisted she take them down in long-
hand, so that he could constantly look over her shoulder to
see what he had said.

In 1962 Langlois did a show of Méliès drawings, sets, and
stills at the Louvre. At least that's what Mary kept saying:
"Darling, we're going to be in the Louvre." Technically she
was right; the show was put on in a wing of the Louvre Palace, but it was not the Musée du Louvre, but rather the Musée des Arts Décoratifs, which is also in the Louvre Palace.

The night before the show was to open, I went along to see
how things were going. At midnight, Langlois stepped back,
looked around the central room, mused, and suddenly declared, "We've got to start all over again. It's all wrong." I
thought he was crazy; it looked fine to me. The carpenters
and other technicians looked grim, realizing that they were
going to be working all night. The next morning at eleven
the show was opened, and when we entered that central room
I realized Langlois had been right: the new arrangement was
infinitely more effective than the one I had seen the night
before. Art critic Annette Michelson wrote that the exhibition was "one of the finest I have ever seen. One wandered
through the reconstitution of a life-work prodigious in its inventive substance as through a forest alive with apparitions
and metamorphoses."[3] But he couldn't have got it right any
sooner: he really did need a deadline.

Nothing pleased Langlois and Mary Meerson more than
discovering new talents. Young men and women would come
to the Cinémathèque offices to show their 16 mm films, and
usually they were screened. Of course, it helped if the filmmaker had some sort of introduction. In 1962, Nestor Almendros, a Cuban refugee who had met Langlois when he helped
transform the Havana Film Club into the Cuban Cinematheque and who had been in Paris for a couple of years as a

"pseudo-student," got up the courage to take his film *Gente en la Playa* (*People of the Beach*), which he had smuggled out of Cuba, to the Cinémathèque. A private screening was organized in the Courcelles building.

> Mary Meerson decreed, "It's cinema verité," and she immediately phoned Jean Rouch, the "leader" of the movement. For once he wasn't in Africa, and he saw and liked my film. He even selected it to be screened at the Musée de l'Homme, and got me invited to an ethnographical festival in Florence. I came back to Paris, thinking that my day had come and that I would be able to start working right away in the French cinema.[4]

It wasn't quite that easy, but within two years Nestor Almendros started his French career working on an episode film called *Paris Seen by . . .*, for which he was lighting cameraman for the spisodes by Jean Douchet and by Eric Rohmer. From then on, he began to shoot all Rohmer's films, and then later most of Truffaut's, until he attained international fame (and an Oscar) for his work on Terence Malick's *Days of Heaven*.

M uch as I admired, even loved, Langlois, I realized then that I could never work *for* him. With him, yes. But to work at the Cinémathèque meant that you had to give up any idea of a private life: you had always to be ready if Henri needed you. *He* had no private life; he and Mary lived entirely for the Cinémathèque, and they couldn't understand why anyone else should be any different. Henri must have realized how I felt, or have known that it wouldn't work, for in spite of all he did for me over the years, he never offered me a job.

At least, I don't think he did. Once in the mid-sixties he asked if I minded telling him how much money I earned at the British Film Institute. I told him, and he shook his head, as if dismissing some thought from his mind. Was he at that point going to suggest I come work with him? It's possible: that head shaking only pointed up what I already knew—that although the salaries at the BFI were not lavish, they were much higher than anything Langlois could afford.

Of course, I sometimes had dinner with Langlois, rather than lunch, but then Mary would come along and she tended to dominate the conversation: if Langlois was paternal with me, Mary was maternal with both of us. But from 1962, all such dinners were devoted to discussing a major new development: the approaching opening of a new theater in the Palais de Chaillot. The rue d'Ulm was to continue, and with a second theater there would be six films a night to program instead of three. Opening shows would have to be found that would impose Chaillot on the Cinémathèque regulars and attract a new and larger audience. Eating seemed to bring out the best in both of them: solutions to old problems were suddenly found; new ideas would come to mind. Everything was subordinated to what Langlois and Mary thought would be the turning point in the history of the Cinémathèque.

8

The State vs. Henri Langlois

The Cinémathèque's splendid new auditorium in the Palais de Chaillot opened in June 1963. The foundations of the palace had been begun by Napoleon, and the auditorium was situated there.

Langlois gave credit to Mary Meerson for obtaining this locale; for one thing, she knew the influential architect who had designed the building in 1937, M. Carlu. But without the help of André Malraux, de Gaulle's Minister of Culture, not even Mary Meerson could have persuaded the government to spend money to build the auditorium.

A PASSION FOR FILMS

The opening was grand indeed. The Garde Républicaine lined the halls and stairways; the corridors were decorated with paintings by Gino Severini, a tapestry by Fernand Léger, and a sculpture by Jean Arp. The poster was designed by Victor Vasarely, and there was even supposed to be a drop curtain by Joan Miró, but it never arrived.

The importance of the Chaillot auditorium cannot be underestimated. First of all, it marked the return of the Cinémathèque to the Right Bank, away from the Bohemian ghetto of the Latin Quarter. Second, the Cinémathèque was now functioning in, and as, a national monument. Finally, the auditorium, with its gorgeous apple-green carpet, the most comfortable seats in Paris, an enormous screen, and the latest projection equipment (16 mm, 35 mm, 70 mm), was at last worthy of the films the Cinémathèque showed. It was much bigger than the rue d'Ulm theater; it had 430 seats—a far cry from the days of the avenue de Messine with its fifty seats. With hindsight we can see that the new auditorium was one cause of the problems that would beset Langlois in the sixties. As long as he was tucked away in a back street in the Latin Quarter, no one was envious; but with the promotion to Chaillot, the Cinémathèque became a much more tempting prize. Chaillot could not have come into existence without massive aid from the state, which, after pouring a lot of money into the auditorium, felt that it should have a greater say in how the Cinémathèque was run.

Langlois inaugurated the new auditorium with a triple-header. First, because the idea of the Cinémathèque as a museum was always in his mind, the theater opened with an exhibition devoted to the work of Étienne-Jules Marey, the French scientist who was one of the major figures of film prehistory. Marey (1830–1904) invented the so-called photographic rifle—an instrument that could take a series of photographs one tenth of a second apart, and thus show for the first time how people and animals moved. He was not a filmmaker in any sense that we now understand the phrase; like the word of Eadweard Muybridge in California, however, his experiments paved the way for the cinema. Marey's "chronophotography" also had great influence on painting, and Langlois demonstrated this by including works by Gino Severini, Max Ernst, and Marcel Duchamp in the exhibition.

For the inauguration of the auditorium proper, Langlois mounted two spectacular shows: one was called "Initiation into American Cinema," the other "Initiation into Japanese Cinema." The shows ran simultaneously, the Japanese from June to August, the American from June to October. Each was the fruit of Langlois's collaboration over the years with Eastman House in Rochester and James Card for the American show, and with the Japanese Film Library and Mrs. Kawakita for the other. In fact, the American show was subtitled "A Tribute to George Eastman House" and the Japanese show "A Homage to the Japanese Film Library." Both were presented "under the high patronage of Monsieur André Malraux, Minister for Cultural Affairs."

The new auditorium was to begin by showing three films a night (later it added a regular matinee at 3 p.m.) and the Cinémathèque also continued to use the rue d'Ulm theater, so one had a choice of six (later seven) films every day,* a choice that had never before existed anywhere. At Chaillot, as at the rue d'Ulm and the avenue de Messine, each film was shown only once. There was only very occasionally advance notice of the screenings: usually they were announced week by week as a public service by newspapers and magazines.

*As if this were not enough, midnight screenings were added on occasion at Chaillot.

For big shows like the Japanese and American ones, booklets were printed with information about the films, but not
the date on which each would be shown. The enormous number of films (there were 130 in the Japanese program and 250
in the American program) put great strain on the functioning
of the Cinémathèque, and one got used to arriving at Chaillot
or the rue d'Ulm to find that the film announced had been
canceled. Usually, the replacement turned out to be equally
interesting. Nor were the foreign films always presented with
French subtitles, or indeed any subtitles at all. But that didn't
seem to matter; from its opening day the Chaillot auditorium
was more popular than anyone had expected.

In spite of all the work involved in the opening and programming of Chaillot, Langlois still found time for other
things. Because I was busy preparing the first New York Film
Festival, I arranged for Tom Milne, assistant editor of *Sight
and Sound,* to go to Paris to prepare a season of French films
called "The Real Avant-Garde," to include films that had not
been seen in Britain for forty years: Feuillade's *Les Vampires*
complete, and excerpts from *Fantômas* and *Judex*; Gance's *Au
Secours!* and *Napoléon*; Léonce Perret's *L'Enfant de Paris*, and
Renoir's *Nana*. Even though Langlois and Mary Meerson
were up to their necks with Chaillot, Milne got all the
screenings he needed to select the films and to write the program notes. The London season was a triumph; its greatest
success was the screening of *Les Vampires*, which began on
Saturday afternoon at four o'clock and lasted, with an inter-
mission for refreshment, until eleven o'clock. Almost everyone stayed. Rarely have I heard such enthusiastic applause as
at the end. As Milne wrote in his introduction to the series,
"This is more than a season of dead films. After half a century
they came as a revelation." That revelation was the work of
Langlois and the Cinémathèque.

ABOVE LEFT: Henri Langlois's mother, Annie-Louise.
ABOVE RIGHT: Langlois's father, Gustave.

Langlois as a young man.
Photographs courtesy André and Danièle Rosch.

Langlois (left) and
Georges Franju in the
early 1930s.
*Courtesy Cinémathèque
Française.*

Musidora as Irma Vep in
Feuillade's *Les Vampires.*
*Courtesy Film Society of
Lincoln Center.*

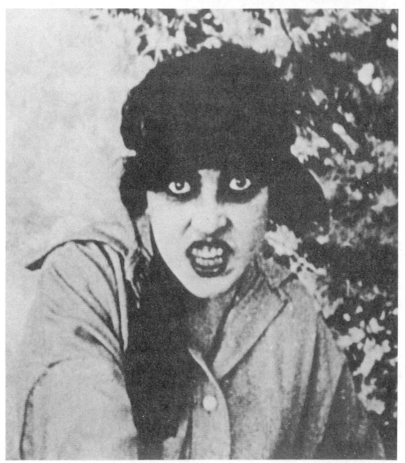

Mary Meerson, ca. 1940
Courtesy Eila Hershon and
Roberto Guerra.

Iris Barry, ca. 1940.
Courtesy Museum of
Modern Art.

Langlois at the National Film Theatre, London, 1969.
Courtesy P.I.C. Photos Ltd.

LEFT: Lotte Eisner (left) with Mary Meerson. *Courtesy Basil Wright.*

BELOW: On the set of *Stolen Kisses*: François Truffaut, Jean-Pierre Léaud, Langlois.

During shooting of *The Wild Child*: Truffaut, Marcel Berbet (producer), Langlois, and Jean-Pierre Cargol, the star. *Photographs courtesy Films du Carosse.*

Louise Brooks in 1928: Paramount publicity photo.

Louise Brooks in 1964.
Photographs courtesy Louise Brooks.

Langlois (center)
and André
Malraux (at left)
at an exhibition
in honor of
Charles Pathé
at the
Cinémathèque,
1959. *Courtesy
Cinémathèque
Française.*

Gloria Swanson
with Langlois
at the
Cinémathèque,
1974. *Photo
© 1974 by Pepe
Diniz.*

Langlois receiving the special Oscar from Jack Valenti as Gene Kelly
looks on: Hollywood, 1974. *Courtesy Cinémathèque Française.*

The State vs. Henri Langlois

☐

The New York Film Festival was organized by Lincoln Center for the Performing Arts in association with the British Film Institute. It began in 1963, and for its first seven years of existence was a twin of the London Film Festival; I programmed both. The first year there were no retrospectives at Lincoln Center, but it was decided in 1964 to have one such program, and I had my heart set on Buñuel's *L'Age d'Or*, never before shown (legally, at least) in New York. Langlois was eager to help, and since the right to show the film had been delegated to him by the original producer (the Vicomte de Noailles), he agreed to send it. But *L'Age d'Or* lasts just over an hour: something else was needed to make up a program. The program booklet for that year says only, "To be announced" for the other part of the *L'Age d'Or* program. It turned out to be a montage, made by Langlois, of new prints of some of the best of his Lumière films. Langlois had a laboratory near Nîmes which was able to make prints from the original negatives, even though they were buckled and shrunken, by printing frame by frame. A long and tedious job, and an expensive one—but instead of looking like old home movies, as they usually did, they were revealed in all their pristine beauty.

The screening of the Lumière montage was instructive. The large audience had come for *L'Age d'Or*, and many of them grew impatient with the montage: there was no story, of course, and the structure was not apparent. Langlois had come over for the screenings, and I remember walking out of Philharmonic Hall halfway through the Lumière film, annoyed and saddened by the audience's reaction. Langlois—who had been in and out of the hall as well—met me on the Grand Promenade and asked why I looked so glum. I told him that I was upset that some of the audience were giggling and others getting restless. "You shouldn't be upset," he said. "Were you inside, when the title came up on the screen that the next film was going to be shots of Loïe Fuller doing her flame dance?" (Loïe Fuller was an American dancer who took Paris by storm around 1900 with her spectacular stage lighting and her "skirt" dancing; she had modeled for Rodin.) "Yes," I said. "Well, didn't you hear a kind of sharp intake of breath, a kind of gulp of surprise and excitement that they were at last actually going to see footage of this legendary dancer?" "Yes, I heard it, but that was less than ten percent of the audience." Langlois wagged his finger at me and said, "Never forget, you're always programming for ten percent of the audience. Nothing matters as long as you've made those ten percent happy."

So successful had the retrospective show in 1964 been that the following year we had three films from Langlois. Foremost was what many thought was the first American screening of *Les Vampires*—although it turned out that the film had been seen before, but not since 1920. So it was a revelation for New York as it had been for London. The very idea of showing a seven-hour film seemed mad to everyone at Lincoln Center: no one will come, they said, and if they do, they won't stay. They were wrong: people came, some with box lunches, and many stayed (although there was some wandering in and out of the auditorium) to give a long ovation at the end of the film. America had discovered Feuillade.

The second film was the sound version of *The Wedding March*, and the third, Buster Keaton's *Seven Chances*. This was one of the so-called lesser films of Keaton, one of those that Iris Barry had not thought worth preserving. We showed *Seven Chances* on a triple bill called "Buster and Beckett," for the program included a Canadian short starring Keaton called

The State vs. Henri Langlois

The Railrodder, and Alan Schneider's *Film* based on a script by Samuel Beckett and starring Buster Keaton. The shorter films got mixed reactions, but *Seven Chances* was a hit.

The next year it was decided to show Renoir's *La Chienne;* it was announced in the ad and even got into the house program, but we had to cancel. Although the rights had been cleared during the summer, and Lincoln Center had even advanced the money to subtitle the film in English, at the last minute the Hakim Brothers production company paid ten million francs to the publisher of the play on which the film was based in order to buy the remake rights. (It had already been remade once, by Fritz Lang, under the title *Scarlet Street*). Langlois could have ignored this new development and sent us the print, but he was afraid that the film itself would suffer. Had we shown it, the Hakim Brothers would have had the right to insist on destroying the print and even the original negative. Langlois did not want to run the risk. The Hakims never did produce their remake, but they abandoned the idea only after trying to interest a number of directors in the project, all of whom refused, not wishing to compete with both Renoir and Lang.

Meanwhile, I continued to program the National Film Theatre in London for eight months of the year, and the last big season I did there with Langlois was a tribute to Abel Gance in 1965. Here was a great director who might be totally unknown today if the Cinémathèque had not collected prints of his films, a debt that Gance acknowledged in an article in *Le Monde* in 1968: "It is thanks to Langlois that some of my earlier films were saved from destruction: *Mater Dolorosa, The Tenth Symphony, Les Gaz Mortels, The Right to Life, Barberousse*, and especially *La Roue* in its 10,000 meter version. More important still, my 1927 *Napoléon*, all 26 reels with the final triple-screen sequence, would have disappeared had it not been for Henri Langlois."[1] Because Langlois had saved all these films and showed them, the young directors of the New Wave were able to "discover" Gance during the 1950s, and Rivette, Truffaut, and Godard were able to discover not only that Gance was the great director of *Napoléon* and *La Roue*—those films were in the history books—but that he had gone on to make important films during the sound period. The second New York Film Festival and the eighth London Film Festival showed Gance's last feature film, *Cyrano et d'Artagnan*, with no great success. I still think it's a wonderful film, but the English subtitled print made specially for us has disappeared. Perhaps if we had been able to show it after the Gance retrospective it would have been better appreciated. In any case, the Gance show in London in 1965 astonished many people, and it was repeated in New York in 1967 as a "Special Event" in the library/museum of Lincoln Center.

This was the first attempt at a major retrospective series in the festival; we showed eight films in the library, and in Philharmonic Hall we screened the Cinémathèque's longest print of *Napoléon*. Its great success started that reevaluation of Gance in America which reached its apex fourteen years later when the full-length *Napoléon*, with the final triptych and accompanied by a symphony orchestra, sold out nine performances in Radio City Music Hall and then went on to tour the country. This print was a painstaking reconstruction by the British filmmaker and historian Kevin Brownlow, using material from the Cinémathèque Française, the National Film Archive in London, and various other sources. At twenty-frames-per-second projection speed (at which the film was originally screened at the Paris Opera House premiere in 1927) the film ran for five hours when shown in London. It was, however, screened in America at twenty-four frames per second, so it only ran for four hours. (The American release version in the late twenties was only a digest: it ran for eighty minutes.)

During this period, Langlois and the Museum of Modern Art in New York reached a temporary rapprochement. Their relationship had deteriorated after Iris Barry left and Richard Griffith became the head of the film department. The two men did not have much esteem for each other. Langlois thought Griffith was lazy and not sufficiently interested in cinema; it is true that in those days, the museum generally showed the same film all week long, usually a classic from its collection. Griffith, on the other hand, was openly contemptuous of Langlois: "That man," he once spluttered to me, "he's not an archivist, he's not a historian, he's just a . . . just an *enthusiast.*" When I told Langlois about it, the idea that enthusiasm could be thought of as a pejorative quality amused him greatly—and proved, as he said, that he was right to despise Griffith. When Willard Van Dyke took over the Museum of Modern Art film department in 1966, Langlois became more cordial, and in 1967 the museum and the Cinémathèque presented a program in New York to celebrate thirty years of film exchanges between the two organizations. The show was devoted to American films from the Cinémathèque collections, films which had disappeared in the United States. At the same time, Langlois arranged a show in Paris of rare American films from the collection of the Museum of Modern Art.

Meanwhile, to the outside world, everything seemed to be going well for Langlois and the Cinémathèque Française. The state had paid for the new theater at the Palais de Chaillot. It had advanced a large sum of money (2,400,000 francs) for making new prints, and Langlois was able to hire a bright young man named Bernard Martinand to help in the programming.

"Help" was the operative word. Langlois enjoyed the weekly stint of programming; he would sit with Martinand (later with Simon Mizrahi) and lay out a blank sheet of graph paper in front of him. His great joy was to establish an evening's screenings so that the film shown at 6:30 would have some hidden connection with the film at 8:30 and the one at 10:30—nothing obvious like the same director or the same stars or even the same studio or the same country. He didn't care whether the audience noticed a connection, for he was sure that unconsciously they would learn from the juxtapositions—a form of montage. Martinand would of course make suggestions, some of which would be howled down with a scream of rage only to be tacitly accepted and inscribed a quarter of an hour later.

Martinand would also have to find out if the films Langlois had chosen were in fact available and not on loan to some foreign archive or promised to one of the Friends-of-the-Cinémathèque film societies in the French provinces. Martinand would also have to check in which vaults a film was stored and make up the delivery-van list—so many films to come from Bois d'Arcy, so many from the deposit in Les Lilas (a suburb of Paris), etc. Films were also borrowed from other archives and from commercial distributors. There was inevitably a great deal of scratching out and replacement, and the program was never ready to be mimeographed and sent to the weeklies which printed the Cinémathèque's schedules until the last possible minute. In the earlier days Langlois had done all this work himself. Now, thanks to the aid of the state, he had someone to help him.

But this largesse had strings attached. In 1964, the government decided that it deserved to be better represented in the functioning of the Cinémathèque. The first step was to add eight state-chosen representatives to the administrative council, originally composed of eight elected members of the general assembly of the Cinémathèque, whose members included anyone who had ever given a film or an artifact (script, poster, etc.) to the Cinémathèque. In theory, the assembly met once a year, but all the members could not attend (many were foreign), so a system of proxies was developed whereby Langlois or Meerson would be in the happy position of voting for as many as eighty or ninety people, thus having a strong influence on the election of the administrative council.

Then sixteen more members of the administrative council were chosen, half by the old members and half by the new ones; these last eight had also to be approved by the state. But the biggest blow to Langlois came from the decision to split his job in two; in 1964 Langlois, who had officially been secretary-general, became artistic and technical director, and a certain Claude Fabrizio was "parachuted" into the Cinémathèque as administrative and financial director. Officially and hierarchically, their posts were equal. Fabrizio was a pleasant young man with little experience of the cinema but with a solid grounding in administration. Whatever his qualities, however, it was an impossible situation. The division between artistic and technical direction and administrative and financial direction was artificial, since almost any artistic or technical decision must affect finances and administration, and vice versa. After so many years of independence Langlois did not take well to the presence of someone theoretically of the same rank as himself in the Cinémathèque.

My first inkling that real trouble was brewing came after the 1964 Cannes Festival when Langlois began to complain that he was obliged to justify every franc he spent. At first I thought he was exaggerating, but when I read the notorious

Heilbronner Report, I realized the situation was even worse than he had suggested. M. Heilbronner was an inspector of finances, and in April 1965, at the request of the Ministry of Finance and Economic Affairs, he submitted a long paper on the workings of the Cinémathèque. This thick mimeographed document was composed of three different-colored papers: the first color was for Heilbronner's objections. The second contained Langlois's responses, and the third Heilbronner's evaluation of Langlois's argument. Occasionally, he would accept Langlois's explanations; more often he would not. It was in any case an unfair and misleading document. Langlois had submitted a modest bill for his expenses at the Cannes Festival of 1964—taxis in Cannes, five dollars; various tips, four dollars; extras and tips at the hotel, five dollars; and drinks offered to "personalities," three dollars, making a grand total of seventeen dollars. These expenses were questioned because, the report said, he had no receipts for them. This was an obvious attempt at harassment: Who asks a hotel porter to give him a receipt for a tip?

But this was only the beginning; the Cinémathèque, Heilbronner reported, was not organized in a rational way. There were no "organigrammes"—charts which showed the exact duties of each employee and his hierarchical relation to the other employees. Furthermore, the inspector observed, the division of responsibility between Langlois and Fabrizio was not always respected: Langlois used his position on the Cinémathèque's administrative council to get many members to give him their proxy. Some of the reproaches were of course valid: there was no proper inventory of the collection. The catalog was, Heilbronner claimed (although how could he know?) twenty-five thousand file cards behind. Most of the complaints, however, showed a lack of understanding as to how the Cinémathèque—or indeed any other film archive—

functioned. Heilbronner made much of the fact that the Cinémathèque spent large sums of money on receptions and entertaining—completely unjustifiable for an organization "whose aim is not public relations but the conservation of an artistic patrimony." He didn't realize that these receptions and the hospitality Langlois offered directors and actors were usually translated almost immediately into gifts of films to the collection, films which otherwise would have cost money or simply have been unavailable. Langlois maintained that it was cheaper to invite directors to Paris for a reception than to make prints or acquire noncommercial screening rights. After Vincente Minnelli was honored by the Cinémathèque, he gave them seventeen prints.

Heilbronner's most ridiculous complaints concerned the use of the Boyer Laboratories near Nîmes for printing the Lumière films mentioned earlier. Heilbronner seemed completely unaware of how difficult it is to make prints from sixty-year-old negatives: all he could see was that the Boyer lab charged thirty-two to thirty-five centimes a meter to print films, whereas Kodak only charged thirty centimes a meter. It's as if someone told Richard Avedon to get his photographs developed at the local drugstore. Heilbronner also complained that Langlois had no written agreements from producers or rights holders for the Cinémathèque screenings. Langlois in his official reply stated that he had tacit agreements which had only to be confirmed by a phone call, and that, since he had the confidence of the Motion Picture Association of America, he was pretty much covered all around. Heilbronner's rejoinder was that such an arrangement was "not satisfactory": Cinémathèque screenings should not have to depend on the tolerance of producers, and a mandatory deposit scheme would be more desirable. Perhaps, but the American companies, as well as the others, were not prepared to sink millions into making a print of each of their films to deposit in the Cinémathèque. Those who contend that "legal deposit"* of films is justifiable on the analogy of the legal deposit of books by publishers in the national libraries forget that a print of a film costs over a hundred times the price of a book. Another uninformed accusation was that the percentage of seats filled at Chaillot and the rue d'Ulm was too low: in 1965, for example, the percentage at the rue d'Ulm was forty-five and at Chaillot thirty-six. If one knows nothing about the film business, this does indeed sound bad—and yet it is higher than that of any commercial cinema in the Western world. Curiously, Langlois did not use this argument; he simply replied that the Cinémathèque had a duty to show little-known and unpopular films, too: such "unpopular" films often found an audience over a period of years.

The Heilbronner Report was only the beginning of a campaign of harassment of the Cinémathèque from 1964 to 1968. Indeed, this was part of a general attempt of the de Gaulle government to centralize the arts and, as François Truffaut said, to institute a measure of thought control. For example, under de Gaulle's Minister of Finance, Michel Debré, film production companies which had previously been allowed to set up shop with a capital of ten thousand dollars were now obliged to have sixty thousand. Why? Truffaut claims that it was because the government wanted to concentrate the film-production business. There were to be fewer producers, fewer distributors; those few would be, on the one hand, more powerful and, on the other, more easily subject to the control of the government. In other words, an attempt to reduce the number of cheeses, as expressed in de Gaulle's famous remark,

---

*And legal deposit would have applied only to *French* films, in any case.

The State vs. Henri Langlois

"How can you govern a country that has more than four hundred registered cheeses?"

Malraux protected Langlois from the worst of the government's attacks for a while but gradually began to turn against him. Some said—and Langlois believed this, too—that it wasn't Malraux's fault: he was badly counseled by his advisers. Others put the blame squarely on Malraux. Truffaut says simply that he wasn't cut out to be Minister of Culture. Others, like Godard, went further, outraged not only by Malraux's treatment of Langlois but by the scandalous banning by the Minister of Information (M. Bourges) of Jacques Rivette's film *Suzanne Simonin, Diderot's Nun*—a banning which overruled the regular censorship board that had passed the film. After Godard had tried unsuccessfully to intervene, he wrote an open letter to Malraux: "Your refusal to see me and answer the phone opened my eyes. What I thought was courage on your part when you saved my *Femme Mariée* from the ax I understand was only cowardice now that I see you are accepting the ban on *La Réligieuse* [the original title of the Rivette film]. It's really sinister to see a Gaullist minister in 1966 afraid of an Encyclopedist [Diderot] of 1789. You won't understand why, in this letter, I am speaking to you for the last time, nor why henceforth I won't shake your hand."

This "open letter" appeared in the *Nouvel Observateur* in April 1966; earlier, in January, when Godard opened the Lumière retrospective at the Cinémathèque, he had remarked on the "wretched treatment" being meted out to Langlois by the government on an occasion placed under the "high patronage" of Malraux himself, particularly pointing out the government's "grudging the price of a few Lumière prints, whose incredible luminosity will shortly astonish you. He is reproved over his choice of laboratory, whereas no one would dream of haggling over the colors used by artists of the School of Paris when they repaint the ceiling of the Opera"[2] (a reference to Malraux's commissioning from Chagall a new mural on the ceiling of the Paris Opera House).

Of course, for someone trained in administrative procedures Langlois was especially difficult to deal with. Wily and secretive, he had always been convinced that there were "spies" within the Cinémathèque. The Argentinian filmmaker Nelly Kaplan found herself suddenly persona non grata because Langlois and Mary had taken it into their heads that she was a Vatican spy. When I innocently protested, "But, Henri, why would the Vatican want to spy on the Cinémathèque, and why would they use someone like Nelly, who is Jewish?" The answer was ready: "Of course they are spying— they're dying to know what films I've got. And why a Jewess? To put us off the track, obviously." There could be no answer to such conviction. One day in the early sixties, I began talking to him about a new show he was planning, and he turned on me in fury, saying, "Who told you that? Who? I *knew* there were spies in the building." "But, Henri," I said, "*you* told me yesterday, yourself." "Oh," was all he said. Now, Fabrizio's function as administrative and financial director was precisely to "spy out" what was going on and to report back to the ministry.

But Marc Allégret (film director and president of the Cinémathèque during the sixties) in his April 1967 report to Malraux supported Langlois. He admitted the need for economy, but he wanted constructive savings, not the kind that were asphyxiating the Cinémathèque. "However unconventional the Cinémathèque's methods might seem," he said, "they *work.*" By 1962, he pointed out, the number of films in its possession had doubled, and by 1967 tripled. At the end of 1962, the Cinémathèque was programming about nine hundred films; by 1964, more than two thousand films were shown each year. Up to 1964 the box office at the rue d'Ulm and Chaillot increased each year; between 1965 and 1967, thanks to the government's constant sniping, they dropped sharply. Because the government stopped its subsidy for making new prints at the end of 1965, and because invitations to foreign filmmakers had been severely curtailed, there was a drop in prestige, publicity, and attendance.

Allégret concluded that apparently every initiative of the Cinémathèque Française, each decision of its council or its president aimed at allowing the Cinémathèque to maintain and safeguard its mission, was countered by maneuvers on the part of the government to render unrealizable every possible decision. He pleaded for funds to establish the long-planned Museum of the Cinema and begged the government to recognize that the Cinémathèque was not being run for private ends. "If the Cinémathèque needs an administrator," he said, "it needs an animator even more, which is why the constant interference of the government in the internal affairs of the Cinémathèque must stop."[3]

As we shall see, Allégret's report went unheeded.

But Langlois was not so involved with his government battles and financial restrictions that he was unable to operate. Although the subsidy to make new prints dried up in 1965, Langlois had already managed to make or get enough new ones to make some stunning revelations. In 1967, he staged an almost complete Howard Hawks retrospective.

Hawks had been a favorite of his ever since he saw Louise Brooks in A Girl in Every Port. As Joseph McBride put it, "Langlois deserves special credit for his work in preserving (and showing) many of Hawks' films. If it hadn't been for Langlois, future critics would never be able to fill in the gaps Andrew Sarris came up against when he wrote his 8,000-word monograph, The World of Howard Hawks, in 1961 and 1962.

A PASSION FOR FILMS

Sarris had not been able to see silent films such as *Fig Leaves* and *A Girl in Every Port*, nor some of the early sound films."[4] But French critics—especially those who were to turn film-makers themselves—were luckier; Rivette, Truffaut, Rohmer, Godard, and Chabrol were all tremendously influenced by the Hawks films. As Rivette put it, "Hawks taught the *Cahiers* school 'all that is best in the classical American cinema,' particularly inspiring them with his ability to personalize the diverse genres in which he worked." Not for nothing did the Young Turks of the *Cahiers* school refer to themselves as *"Hitchcocko-Hawksians."*

For years, however, Langlois's attitude toward Hawks was considered incomprehensible by American critics and curators. When Langlois visited America for the first time in 1939, he kept asking people whether they had seen this great film, *Only Angels Have Wings*, only to meet with looks of bafflement or amused tolerance. No, of course, they hadn't seen it—it was a commercial Hollywood product. As late as 1962, when Shirley Clarke came to Paris to show *The Connection*, she said to me wonderingly, "You know, Langlois asked me whether I had ever seen *Only Angels Have Wings*. I said I may have seen it as a child, but I didn't remember it. Why do you think he thinks it's so good? It's just another Hollywood film, isn't it?" Well, no, I said, it isn't. . . . A year later, Clarke had caught up with the film, on television, and she had to agree that Langlois had been right.

Similarly, Langlois said in the early 1960s that people in New York used to ask him why Europeans were so interested in the films of Nicholas Ray and Joseph Losey. "I think that time has proved Europe right, just as it proved Europe right on Sjöström's *The Wind* and Fejos's *Lonesome*. On the other hand," Langlois added, "there are French films which are more appreciated in America than in France, and in these instances, New York is right." (The most dramatic case was that of Marcel Pagnol, who was underrated in France for years when large American audiences were enjoying *The Baker's Wife* and the *Marius-Fanny-César* trilogy.)

The French love for Hawks became, through constant screenings at the Cinémathèque, almost unconditional. Almost, I say, because there was a night in the 1967 Hawks retrospective when Langlois showed a brand-new print of *His Girl Friday*. The print had no subtitles, and one must remember that this is perhaps the fastest-talking film in the history of American cinema. The audience was very excited before the performance, and even into the first reel or two. But even those with a fair knowledge of English were not able to keep up with the constant stream of wisecracks, and the mood of the audience grew restless, almost mutinous. I thought of the sequence in the Marx Brothers film *Duck Soup* when Groucho is handed a letter, which Harpo grabs from him, opens, looks at, and then tears up in a fit of rage. Why did he do that, asks Groucho of Chico, who explains: "He gets mad because he can't read." The audience knew they were missing something—especially because some English or American people in the audience were laughing constantly.

Sometimes Langlois was able to do things outside Paris that were impossible there for financial reasons. Whenever he was offered the money to arrange a retrospective or an exhibition abroad or in the provinces he seized the opportunity. One of the most spectacular of these came in 1966 at the Cannes Film Festival. The locale he was offered was bizarre: the Grand Ballroom of the Hôtel Martinez. The aim of the show, as Langlois announced, was not only to celebrate the seventieth anniversay of the Lumières' show in December

1895 but also to present some of the riches discovered and preserved by the Cinémathèque in preparation for his long-dreamed-of *"grand musée du cinéma"* which was planned for Chaillot.

Given the space that Langlois had at his disposal, there was no question of a chronological show—the ballroom was too vast and not easily divisible. So he adopted the solution found by the Louvre after the Liberation of Paris when it showed in a few large rooms, pell-mell, its most important treasures, mixing up the primitives with the Impressionists, Ingres with Memling. The result was that, as Langlois put it, the only thread leading through the labyrinth was the unity of film art. The exhibits at the Martinez were grouped by affinities: historical films, expressionist films, Futurist films, the world of slapstick, etc. Langlois also tried to show the links between films like *Fantômas* and the James Bond series, between Victorin Jasset's *Protéa* and Losey's *Modesty Blaise*. He was a past master at the art of juxtaposition (which in a sense is an art of the cinema: montage), so we saw stills, costumes, and set designs from *Caligari* next to artifacts from *The Lady from Shanghai*, Dreyer's *Passion de Jeanne d'Arc* next to Bresson's *Procès de Jeanne d'Arc*. Langlois showed the universality of the art of the cinema and gave a hint of what the future Museum of the Cinema was to be.

When I arrived in Cannes that year Langlois immediately dragooned me into helping him. The opening was scheduled for the next morning, and, although he had planned the exhibit months in advance, nothing was ready, or so it seemed. My job, Langlois decreed, was to prepare labels: he realized that I wasn't good at manual work. So until I gave up at four in the morning, I was typing out labels while a team of press-ganged friends and associates were hammering away, hanging things, waiting while Langlois examined the result and then decided that no, this still must go over there, only to change his mind later and decide that really the place it had first been hung was the best after all. I had seen two of Langlois's shows before (the Méliès show at the Louvre, and the big show at the Musée National d'Art Moderne), but by the time I went to bed—a bare seven hours before this one was to be inaugurated—it still looked a mess, and I was convinced that for once he had bitten off more than he could chew.

I was wrong. When I arrived the next morning the mess of the night before had been miraculously transformed into something quite wonderful. As Penelope Houston wrote:

> Stills and posters; scripts, sketches, costumes, mechanical gadgets. In its cunning air of disarray, the exhibition enchantingly reflected the image one has of the Cinémathèque's own personality, as a kind of magpie nest with Henri Langlois roosting at its centre. Crumpled, grimy, and forlorn, the old costumes—Stroheim's *Wedding March* uniform, Cherkassov's huge boots for *Ivan the Terrible*, Vivien Leigh's grey and green (wasn't it once white and green?) dress for *Gone With the Wind*, even all those beaded evening dresses—carried a surprisingly powerful nostalgic charge. Among the scripts, one noted Satyajit Ray's neat little drawings, Godard's scrawled capitals, the startlingly illiterate hands of many of the great. I can't remember a more attractive exhibition in this line, and one wishes it could be brought to London. Keaton's hat; a death mask of Mizoguchi; a torn Griffith contract, unexpectedly touching relics from the art which used to think it had no history.[5]

In spite of these triumphs, the government was closing in on Langlois. He had not convoked a Cinémathèque general assembly between 1964 and 1967. Marc Allégret's report of

April 1967 had been ignored, and the minister of finance blocked all payment of subsidies "until the Cinémathèque was reorganized."

Sensing the danger, Langlois brought Jean Riboud, chief executive officer of the multinational oil-drilling Schlumberger company, onto the administrative council. The two men had met in 1958 when Riboud's Indian wife, Krishna, was on the shorts jury at the Cannes Film Festival. They became close friends; Langlois and Mary spent a lot of time with them in Paris, and Henri used to go to their country house in the Beaujolais. (One summer he arrived with Joris Ivens to spend the night—and they ended up staying a month. Ivens was helping Langlois work on his Chagall film, and the large billiard table in the Riboud house was very useful to them.)

Langlois had discussed his problems with Riboud over the years, but Riboud remained just a friendly adviser until the end of 1967, when Langlois realized that he needed his administrative expertise. On December 18 Riboud accompanied Langlois to a meeting with Malraux and Allégret. According to Riboud, Malraux asked them to help him pacify Michel Debré, Minister of Finance, who was sniping away about the financial disorder of the Cinémathèque. Riboud replied that they would do all they could to help Malraux on two conditions: that the Cinémathèque remain independent, and that Langlois be reinstated as secretary-general. Malraux accepted the conditions. "So," Riboud said, "we agreed to do what he wanted, that is, to give the administrative council's majority to the representatives of the state."

But Malraux did not keep his word. "To be fair," Riboud adds, "Malraux never was a good administrator and was certainly no expert in financial and budgetary matters. Furthermore, there were several government officials who kept pushing Malraux to get rid of Langlois—notably the director of the Centre National du Cinéma, André Holleaux. He was orchestrating the battle against Langlois because he wanted the Cinémathèque to come under the centralizing power of his CNC." Another man, whom Riboud would not identify but who was a member of Malraux's cabinet, also played a "detestable" role in fomenting trouble between Debré and Malraux with only one end in view: to get rid of Langlois and to take over the Cinémathèque. Langlois, after all the years of imagining "plots" against him, was now about to become the victim of a very real one.

9

The Battle for the Cinémathèque

The *affaire Langlois* began on February 9, 1968—and ended on April 22. But one could also say that, just as the *affaire* of the Queen's Necklace was one of the causes of the French Revolution of 1789, so the Langlois crisis didn't really end on April 22, because the "events" of May 1968, as the violent student demonstrations were discreetly called in France, were a logical continuation of it.

On Friday, February 9, there was a meeting of the administrative council of the Cinémathèque Française. Its new president, Pierre Moinot (Director of Arts and Letters in the de Gaulle government), began with an enthusiastic speech in favor of Langlois, but concluded by proposing that Langlois, in his capacity of artistic and technical director of the Ciné-mathèque, be replaced by one Pierre Barbin.

Barbin was not a well-known figure, although he had gained a reputation as a good organizer as the director of two short film festivals in France, one in Tours and one (devoted to animated films) in Annecy. According to Georges Gold-fayn, Barbin had said at the Tours festival in January 1968 that he was soon to become the director of the Cinéma-thèque; producer Pierre Braunberger had heard the same thing. Goldfayn phoned Langlois three hours after hearing this boast, but Langlois took it lightly: yes, he said, he knew there was a vast movement against him. But he seemed re-signed to some change in his status. Still joking, he asked Goldfayn whether he would enjoy working for Barbin.

Those members of the council who were in opposition to the Director of Arts and Letters were astonished at Moinot's proposal, and promptly asked for a week's delay before pro-ceeding to a vote. This waiting period was refused by Moinot, and the members of the council were directed to vote. Before the balloting, André Holleaux announced that André Mal-raux himself had proposed Pierre Barbin and his associate Raymond Maillet as codirectors—Barbin to take over the po-sition of Langlois, and Maillet that of Fabrizio, administrative and financial director. He added that the ministry recognized the importance of Langlois's possible future collaboration in the Cinémathèque and that sometime soon the ministry would make known just what function he would be given.

Profoundly upset by this sudden turn of events, eight of the thirty-two members of the council refused to vote and walked out of the meeting. They were Yvonne Dornès, Denise Le-marisquier, Hubert Devillez, Louis-Émile Galley, Alexandre

Kamenka (who had just been elected first vice-president of the Cinémathèque), Jean Riboud, Ambroise Roux, and François Truffaut. The voting then took place: Barbin and Maillet were elected.

That afternoon, the two new directors, accompanied by what *Cahiers du Cinéma* termed "a little commando force," installed themselves in Langlois's offices on the rue de Courcelles, had the locks on the buildings changed, and delivered a letter of dismissal to Mary Meerson, who was outside on the sidewalk. Marie Epstein was in the Cinémathèque working away, unaware of what had happened, and when she finished, around midnight, she couldn't get out of the building. (Mlle. Epstein, with Langlois's approval, stayed on at the Cinémathèque during the Barbin regime. The reason was obvious for anyone who knew Langlois: he needed someone he trusted totally to inform him about what was going on. Barbin needed her because she knew where everything was.)

M. Holleaux, thinking that the whole affair of the Cinémathèque was settled once and for all, went off on a skiing vacation. He soon had to return.

Saturday, February 10: most of the newspapers not only announced the change but criticized it violently. The battle had begun. Forty filmmakers—among them Gance, Truffaut, Resnais, Franju, Godard, Chris Marker, Alexandre Astruc, Chabrol, Bresson, Renoir, Eric Rohmer, Jean Rouch—not only protested against the Ministry of Culture's decision, but announced that they would not allow their films to be projected by the "Barbinothèque." Within several hours almost the whole of the French cinema mobilized itself to defend Langlois. The *Cahiers du Cinéma* began to send off cables all over the world to encourage foreign filmmakers to join the boycott. For the first time in the history of French cinema, almost all directors of whatever tendency, younger or older

generation, joined together. (There were a few abstentions—
Marcel L'Herbier, Roger Leenhardt, and René Clair.)

The only response from the Direction General des Arts et
des Lettres was an embarrassed communiqué which stated
that the Cinémathèque Française, whose riches were slowly
accumulated by Henri Langlois, had become such an important organization that it was no longer possible for it to be run
in the same amateur way that had been its style over the previous twenty years.

Sunday, February 11: all the Sunday papers took a stand in
favor of Langlois, from the right-wing *Journal du Dimanche* to
the organ of the French Communist Party, *L'Humanité Dimanche*. The *Cahiers* sent out more telegrams, and more an-
swers poured in.

Monday, February 12: what has been described as one of
the longest and most violent press campaigns in the history of
France began with articles by Truffaut, Chabrol, and many
journalists. Truffaut—who had been a brilliant polemicist in
the early days of the New Wave—had lost none of his bite. In
a piece in the morning paper *Combat* he accused André Malraux directly. For too long now, he wrote, people have said
that whenever the Ministry of Culture did something wrong,
it wasn't Malraux's fault but that of Michel Debré, Minister of
Finance. But this time, he wrote, it is quite clear that it was
the decision of Malraux himself to dismiss Langlois.

By now, more than sixty directors had signed the boycott
petition, and even the heirs of directors joined in—the
daughter of Jean Vigo among them, to be followed by a dozen
other heirs and rights holders. The C.G.T., the national federation of trade unions, also took a stand, maintaining that
the dismissal of Langlois was one more confirmation of the
present government's attempt, in cultural affairs as well as
others, to take control.

A PASSION FOR FILMS

But perhaps the most important event of the day was a spontaneous meeting at the rue d'Ulm; from 6 to 10 p.m. two to three hundred filmmakers, critics, film fans, and actors demonstrated in front of the Left Bank screening room. They were there to prevent people from attending the screenings, and they were successful: at the 6:30 showing, there were only seven spectators. Then the responses from abroad began to arrive: Nicholas Ray, Joseph Losey, Robert Florey, Vincente Minnelli, Roberto Rossellini—all forbidding any screenings of their films at the "Barbinothèque."

The most apt protest came from the director Alexandre Astruc, who pointed out that Langlois was to the Cinémathèque what de Gaulle, in the eyes of Gaullists, was to France, and that if directors had given prints to the Cinémathèque, they had not given them to X, Y, or Z, but to Henri Langlois. And, he predicted, after the directors, the distributors would follow suit, and M. Barbin would find himself at the head of an organization which would lack only two things: films and audiences.

Tuesday, February 13: Barbin fired forty employees of the Cinémathèque and declared to Le Figaro, "People are wrong to speak of Langlois's dismissal. It is only a reorganization. And I ardently hope, for my part, that Langlois will come to see that I am a man of good will."

Langlois himself—this was perhaps the cleverest thing he could have done—made no declarations to the press, radio, or television. Indeed, throughout the whole affair he kept silent; he was, however, even busier on the telephone than usual. Truffaut, Godard, Chabrol, and Rouch announced a press conference in the Palais de Chaillot which was held at 6 p.m. on the following day. Meanwhile, more cables from abroad flowed in and were quoted in the newspapers: Fritz Lang, Orson Welles ("MOST DISTRESSED DISMISSAL OF

HENRI LANGLOIS AND PROTEST THIS ARBITRARY ACTION IN STRONGEST POSSIBLE TERMS STOP OF COURSE WILL NOT PERMIT SCREENING OF MY FILMS AT CINEMATHEQUE FRANCAISE UNTIL FURTHER NOTICE") and Charles Chaplain ("IN THE CAUSE OF THE EXCELLENCE OF ART I MUST ADD MY NAME TO THE LIST OF THOSE PROTESTING AGAINST THE DISMISSAL OF HENRI LANGLOIS"). Actors and actresses also protested: Alain Delon, Marlene Dietrich, Simone Signoret, Delphine Seyrig, Yves Montand, Michel Simon (who had spoken at the rue d'Ulm the previous day).

The new directorate announced that they were closing both the Cinémathèque's theaters—Chaillot and rue d'Ulm—because they were "in the process of totally reorganizing the Cinémathèque, and . . . the theaters would be needed for purposes of inventory."

Wednesday, February 14: the day of the billy clubs. Three thousand people in the gardens of the Trocadéro near the Chaillot screening room answered Truffaut's call in the newspaper *Combat*: Everyone to Chaillot for the 6 p.m. meeting. But from 3 p.m., thirty-odd police cars had surrounded the neighborhood to prevent anyone from getting too near the entrance. Television cameras were set up (foreign ones, that is, for none of this was allowed to appear on French television). Tracts were distributed, and the huge group began to move eastward across the gardens toward the Chaillot screening room. They found themselves faced with a police barrage, and no one, except Jean-Luc Godard, got through.

So the group reformed, moved up onto the avenue du Président Wilson, blocking all traffic, and attempted to reach the theater by a different route. When they got to the corner of the avenue Albert-de-Mun, they came upon a new police line.

Then the police charged. Truffaut and Godard were slightly injured, Bertrand Tavernier's face was covered with blood, Anne-Marie Roy had her wrist broken, and others were knocked to the ground. One of them was Helen Scott, an old-time Communist Party organizer. (When Robert Hawkins of *Variety* became upset while helping her to her feet, his colleague Gene Moskowitz reassured him, saying, "Don't worry, she's been through this kind of thing so many times that when you do get her up she'll start screaming, 'Justice for Sacco and Vanzetti!' ")

Around 8 p.m. Godard (who had lost his glasses in the scuffle) gave the order to disperse. But if the crowd dispersed, they were not vanquished. With great prescience, Jean Rouch declared to them that this was the beginning of a cultural revolution, the first consciousness-raising among youth, and a rejection of the government's increasing attempts to regulate and control all elements of French life. To use the words of General de Gaulle himself, the Children of the Cinémathèque had only lost a battle—they had not lost the war. Langlois, said journalist Henri Chapier, had become a symbol, a figure synonymous with freedom.

Meanwhile, the foreign telegrams continued to arrive: Lindsay Anderson, Elia Kazan, Anatole Litvak, Luis Buñuel, Karel Reisz, Samuel Fuller.

Thursday, February 15: the administrative council of the Cinémathèque met, and, according to *Le Monde*, Pierre Moinot announced that he intended to confer important responsibilities on Langlois, thus allowing him to pursue his work. He would offer him the chance to create a museum of cinema, to direct its exhibitions, and to prepare a center of film research and experimentation. This was the first sign of weakening on the government side. Although the Agence France-Presse did its best to minimize the events of the preceding day (there were only a few hundred people, they claimed, and even maintained that some demonstrators had simulated blood on their faces with Mercurochrome), the press remained favorable to Langlois. The police, it was said, were furious with the cultural affairs department for having gotten them into such a messy and unpleasant situation.

Friday, February 16: Truffaut, Godard, Rouch, and Chabrol, who had more or less taken charge of the pro-Langlois movement, decided to organize a systematic boycott. They established a Committee for the Defense of the Cinémathèque Française, with Jean Renoir as honorary president, Alain Resnais president, Henri Alekan and Pierre Kast vice-presidents, Godard and Rivette secretaries, and Truffaut and Jacques Doniol-Valcroze treasurers. At 6 p.m. they held a press conference in a cinema called Studio Action.

So ended the first eight days of the Battle for the Cinémathèque. The weeks that followed were less dramatic. On February 20, there was another demonstration, this time in the rue de Courcelles, with Françoise Rosay and Jean Marais leading several hundred people. That same afternoon, the Agence France-Presse announced that Pierre Barbin would be going to the United States shortly to attempt to set up a legal system by which every producer of every film *shown* in France would be obliged by law to deposit one print with the Cinémathèque Française. Three days later this trip was canceled.

That same day, M. Moinot proposed a visit to the vaults of the Cinémathèque Française at Bois d'Arcy to show the journalists in what bad conditions Langlois kept prints. The next day, *Le Figaro* published two photographs: one of stacks of rusty film cans and one of M. Moinot holding an open film can showing the disintegrated film inside. *Le Monde* charged that this was a "guided tour": the journalists were shown only what the government wanted them to see. Of course, Langlois's supporters knew that the Cinémathèque had a lot of

rusty cans, but they often contained prints in very good condition. Also, *Le Monde* pointed out that since Langlois accepted whatever anyone would give him, it is likely that some
of the films he "preserved" were already disintegrating when
he got them. A "proper" archive would examine every film
can as soon as it came into the vaults, but Langlois had neither the personnel nor the time and money (which comes to
the same thing) to do this. "Without Langlois, there would
be nothing," declared M. Moinot, "but because of him certain films are in a deplorable condition." He did not say how
many.

Malraux, like Langlois, had kept silent since the beginning
of the *affaire*, but on February 24, two weeks after it had begun, he made a statement in the *Journal Officiel* in the form of
a response to written questions from some members of the
Chamber of Deputies. It was the only official government
statement throughout the affair. This is how it began:

"All those who are familiar with the Cinémathèque Française know that its founder and his collaborators are not
adapted to the elementary demands of the administration of
an institution of this kind and of this importance. In particular, the Centre National du Cinéma has never succeeded in
finding out the number and titles of the films which the Cinémathèque possesses, nor on what legal basis they have been
deposited, with regard to possession as well as to use, nor
where they are kept."

This was certainly true—Langlois, with his natural tendency toward secrecy, didn't want the government or anyone to
know exactly what he had. Moreover, he was careful never to
disclose the provenance of many of the films deposited with
him—often for the reason that those who had given him the
films didn't always have the right to do so. Illegality? Yes, but
in Langlois's mind, only temporarily so. To Langlois it was

important that the films be there because one day they would become showable, either because they would enter the public domain or because their legal status would be straightened out. The rest of Malraux's statement simply went over the government's attempts during the preceding years to make the Cinémathèque into a well-run government service. Malraux concluded with the following words: "A collection of books does not become the National Library [Bibliothèque Nationale] without a decisive tranformation. It is the same with the Cinémathèque. Langlois has rendered eminent services. He does well what he likes doing, less well what he doesn't like doing. . . . The list of those whose help he has refused is beginning to be a long one."

From then on Malraux kept silent. Did he know he was beaten? Did he know he was wrong? Or was pressure put on him from other members of the government who had decided that they had better let the whole thing drop? Perhaps, too, as has been suggested even by Barbin's defenders, Barbin was not the right kind of fighter. Faced with a Langlois—whom even Moinot called "a ragpicker of genius"—he may not have had an aggressive enough personality. In any case, he apparently had never dreamed how violent the struggle would be, what passions it would unleash. He probably thought that with the government behind him, nothing could go wrong. And that was the point of the *affaire Langlois*—and why many say that it led to the "events" of May. It showed the French that they could successfully oppose the autocratic government of de Gaulle, Debré, and Malraux.

The fact that two important Soviet filmmakers—Grigori Kozintsev and Sergei Yutkevitch—had protested the dismissal of Langlois and as members of the Cinémathèque had called for a new general assembly did much to help Langlois. But it was the American film companies that really saved him: according to S. Frederick Gronich, the member companies of the MPAA (Paramount, Fox, Warners, et al.) authorized him to call on André Malraux personally when the confrontation had reached fever pitch and to tell him that if he continued with his plan, the American companies would withdraw all their films. "I had already suspended all further delivery of films to the Cinémathèque," Gronich told me, "in anticipation of this visit. Not a foot of film was going in there from any American studio. The American companies, in that sense, are very disciplined. So I simply told Malraux that we would have to seriously consider withdrawing everything."

"Malraux was rather taken aback," Gronich told me. "He had not really understood the problems. He was so heavily involved in creating his *maisons de culture* in the provinces that all he could think of was that the Cinémathèque would be the ideal source for programming them. Films are the biggest magnet; all you've got to do is show them Mickey Mouse and you've got your *maison de culture* filled.

"Then Malraux asked if we were determined to go ahead with our threat. I replied that one doesn't go to see a minister unless one really has made up one's mind. Malraux understood the seriousness of the threat, and that was the end of it. That's what broke the back of the government's opposition to Langlois."

"This visit was never reported in the press, was it?" I asked Gronich.

"No, never," he replied. "It would have looked as if the American film industry had served an ultimatum on the French government."

"But that was in fact just what you did!"

"Well, you could put it that way; I prefer to think of it simply as looking after our property."

Gronich cannot remember what day he visited Malraux,

but it must have been before March 6, because on that date *Le Monde* announced that there would be a new general assembly on April 22, and concluded that this signified a step toward the settlement of the *affaire Langlois*. Did *Le Monde's* editors have an inkling of Gronich's visit? Or had they simply heard from the Malraux cabinet that there was to be a change of direction? In any case, they seem to have sensed that the battle of culture heroes was going to terminate with a victory for Langlois. It's no secret that the French pay great attention to culture heroes. Malraux, of course, had been one—for his novels, his film *Espoir*, his reputation as a Resistance fighter, his mastery of French prose, and his books on art. But in the *affaire Langlois*, many equally important heroes, national and international, were lined up on Langlois's side. There were Aragon, the Communist, and Anouilh, the conservative; there were Roland Barthes, Samuel Beckett, and Simone de Beauvoir; Alexander Calder and Truman Capote; Henri Cartier-Bresson; Marguerite Duras and Shelagh Delaney; Max Ernst, Eugene Ionesco, Pauline Kael, Wilfredo Lam, Pierre Mendès-France, Norman Mailer, Pablo Picasso, Raymond Queneau, Andrew Sarris, Jean-Paul Sartre; Susan Sontag and Elliott Stein; Victor Vasarely and Iannis Xenakis—an impressive international roll call of intellectuals and artists when it was printed in *Cahiers du Cinéma.*

Then, too, in spite of Langlois's battles with FIAF, a number of foreign archives joined in the protest: the Swiss, the Canadians, the Italians, the Japanese, the Russians, the Iranians, the Germans, the film department of the Museum of Modern Art in New York; and there were the festival directors, Venice and New York; there were the Film-Makers Co-operative of New York, the Directors Guild of America, etc., etc.

No government gives in quickly. Face has to be saved, so

A PASSION FOR FILMS

the first solution the government proposed was to split up the Cinémathèque: Holleaux, director of the CNC, said on television as late as April 16 that they were thinking of putting Langlois in charge of programming but someone else in charge of preserving films. This was obviously unacceptable, because the two functions must be interdependent, and on April 18 the Committee for the Defense of the Cinémathèque Française refused this compromise. On Sunday, April 21, the Ministry of Culture announced that the state would withdraw its representation on the administrative council of the Cinémathèque after assuming all its debts. The Cinémathèque would once again belong to its members.

So on Monday, April 22, the general assembly convened, and, after his cleverly self-imposed seclusion, Langlois was reelected secretary-general. The affair was over. Or was it?

With the departure of the government, the money dried up, too. To be sure, the state did continue to fulfill certain responsibilities: it paid for light and heat at Chaillot and a few other things, but by and large the Cinémathèque was left to its own resources. Before Chaillot, before the government encouraged Langlois to think big, Langlois had got along fairly well. Now he would have to spend more time and energy looking for money.

10

Crossing the Atlantic

The first offer of money came from an unlikely source,
Serge Losique, distinguished professor at Sir George Williams University in Montreal. Losique and Langlois had first
met when Losique was a student in Paris in 1950, and by 1952
they had become quite close. Losique left Paris in 1957 and
went to Montreal, and their paths did not cross again until
1967, when Losique became the Cinémathèque's "correspondent" in Montreal. In 1968, as soon as Losique heard the
news of Langlois's dismissal, he phoned him and said, "Langlois, now that they've thrown you out, come to me in Mon-

treal." Langlois's first reaction was negative: "Are you crazy? I'm self-taught; I never even passed my baccalaureate, and you want me to become a professor?" "But," says Losique, "I think he was touched that I was trying to help him on the very day after he was dismissed. I had no authority to make him an offer; I figured I'd get the money from somewhere and then get it past all the committees and the university red tape. He phoned me back a month later and said, 'I've thought it over, and I accept.'

"Of course, he could not start until the fall term of 'sixty-eight. He arrived in September to give his first course, and he kept coming back for three years. He flew over every three weeks, arriving on Thursday night and leaving on Sunday night: three days. He taught a history of the cinema course: there was no strict timetable. In 1968 and 1969, he taught in an auditorium of seven hundred seats—packed. The first day, he said, 'I'm not a professor. I don't know how to teach, so I'll show you Lumière and Méliès.' The students were completely taken aback by his methods until they finally understood that with a Langlois you didn't take notes. Once they realized what he was up to, they didn't want to. They were too fascinated by him and the films he showed them.

"To save the academic side of the thing, we had to have exams. But first he asked them to do practical work. 'You've got cameras; go to the railway station in Montreal, set up your camera, and shoot the arrival of a train in the railway station, just like Lumière did at La Ciotat.' As to written exams, I made them up with Langlois, and I remember we graded them together in a hotel room during the Cannes Festival. It was I who had to actually give the grades. He was completely ignorant of the university world.

"He told me he learned a lot about the cinema from being obliged to teach. The students' questions forced him to think. The courses lasted three hours, and afterwards he would go back with the most interested students, ten or fifteen of them, to his hotel room, where the course continued. It was very tiring for him. On Saturdays he would start at ten in the morning and finish by midnight.

"His arrivals were always dramatic: I had to go to the airport myself every time to get the films he brought with him through customs. Once he arrived with no import papers, and he was arrested: they thought he was a Turkish revolutionary!

"Sometimes we managed to get him a first-class ticket, because for a man his size tourist seats were uncomfortable. He was lucky in one respect: he usually managed to fall asleep even before the plane took off from Orly. He could sleep anywhere, eat anything. But as early as 1968, he was not a well man. He had gout, and his heart was weak. In Montreal he found what he called his country doctor—Dr. Laurier, in whom he had complete confidence. But to come back to the courses: he was fantastic. They were always different; he never repeated himself. After three years, however, he had to stop. I proposed that he come back for three weeks each semester, but he wasn't strong enough; he was too tired. But he loved America, and I mean by that North America—Canada and the U.S. It was his dream; like so many Europeans, he thought of it as the land of the open frontier, the land where everything was possible."

Then came the first American approaches. "I remember an article in the *Washington Post* titled 'Legendary Langlois Is Coming.' What impressed the Americans most, I think, was his stature as an individual who had won out over a strong government, and that contributed enormously to his popularity. He must be a great man because he beat de Gaulle: that's what they thought." Langlois's first American job was a series of lectures at the Smithsonian Institution in Washington. Later he lectured at Harvard.

When Langlois met Tom Johnston and his French wife,

Mireille, at a Thanksgiving dinner in 1968 at the New York home of Nell Cox, the documentary filmmaker, none of them realized what a momentous occasion it was. Miss Cox had known Johnston from back home in Kentucky, and they had also seen a lot of each other when Johnston was working for Drew Associates, the documentary filmmaking team which included Robert Drew, Richard Leacock, and Don Pennebaker. Johnston had been working on The Eye, a nonprofit scheme to show films at a theater across from the United Nations. It was to be a place where short films could be shown: at night a revolving cycle of, say, Brazilian shorts, and in the day, hour-long programs of mixed shorts for tourists who visited the U.N. and then found themselves in a dull part of town with nothing to do. The idea was to use a burned-out Howard Johnson's on Forty-fifth Street—I. M. Pei had even worked on a design, and they were to get money from the Ford Foundation. The only remaining problem seemed to be film supply, and Nell Cox thought that Langlois might be able to help.

Tom Johnston had come to New York in 1962 to work with Drew Associates. In 1963, after President Kennedy was killed, he worked for them on a short film about reactions to the assassination called *Faces in November.* During the making of that film—which was more journalism, he says, than filmmaking—Robert Kennedy decided to run for president in 1968, and Johnston, although he enjoyed filmmaking, preferred to work as a volunteer on Kennedy's campaign. He was soon put in charge of the New York office; he and Kennedy got to know and like each other, and Johnston organized Kennedy's Latin American and African trips. Then he spent a year in New York City's Bedford-Stuyvesant area on an economic development project. Johnston had already started on The Eye when Robert Kennedy was killed in 1968, and he wanted to continue the project. But the source of films was lacking—which is why Nell Cox brought him together with Langlois.

An odder couple would be hard to imagine: Johnston was tall, handsome, obviously from a wealthy background (his full name was Thomas Morrison Carnegie Johnston): very much the New Frontiersman. But they hit it off immediately, and Langlois, in that usual way when he had decided he liked someone, said to Johnston, "I'll give you whatever you want. Let's do it." At subsequent meetings they talked about programming and got to know each other better. But The Eye ran into problems: it had been funded by the Kaplan Foundation originally, and the space was to have been given by the United Nations. They had counted on support from the Ford Foundation as well, and that support did not materialize as quickly as Johnston had expected.

Before starting The Eye, Johnston had decided to learn something about the business end of movies and had attended the Harvard School of Business Administration for several months. He then took a job with Jock Whitney (John Hay Whitney, the well-known publisher and financier).* Whitney had also been closely involved with film. Immensely rich, he had been a prominent and enduring angel for many Broadway productions, and he was a founder of Pioneer Pictures, a company set up to make movies in Technicolor, a process in which Hollywood had little faith at the time. He later joined a partnership known as Selznick International, and was the prime instigator and supporter of Selznick's project to make *Gone With the Wind.* He continued intermittently to be involved with filmmaking, and he was a board member of the

---

*Twenty-odd years earlier he had helped Iris Barry to set up the film department of the Museum of Modern Art.

Museum of Modern Art for forty-six years and its chairman from 1946 to 1956.

The plans for The Eye at the U.N. had not been completely dropped when, in the spring of 1969, Johnston got a call from Willard Van Dyke, director of the film department of the Museum of Modern Art. Johnston had met him already and knew one of his sons. Van Dyke said they had to talk: "You can't do The Eye." "What?" said Johnston, thinking Van Dyke meant that he wasn't up to the job. But no. "You can't work with Langlois in New York any more than I could go to Paris and set up my own operation there." Johnston, thunderstruck, said, "This is New York City. Do you mean to say that you have a franchise for New York, and that you don't want anyone moving in on it," asked Johnston. "Yes," said Van Dyke.

"I don't get it," said Johnston. "There are several ballet companies here and opera companies. Surely you can't think that one organization—yours—is enough to handle film in New York. Furthermore, you don't show that many films per week, and your shows are mostly in the afternoon when many people can't get to the museum. You ought to welcome Langlois. He may be difficult sometimes, but think what he did for Paris: he could do a lot for New York, too."

Van Dyke simply replied that he didn't see any need for The Eye and that it would be positively harmful. "It will undercut our efforts here at the museum." Johnston was convinced that Van Dyke was wrong and told him that they were going to go ahead in spite of his objections. "Thereupon, Van Dyke," says Johnston, "wrote a letter to Jock Whitney and David Rockefeller. Whitney, through Benno Schmidt, managing partner at J. H. Whitney, showed me the letter (Whitney was not only my employer but also a family friend). The letter said, in effect, quoting me out of context, that Langlois was difficult to work with, eliminating the word *sometimes*, and went on to say that he was a disruptive and disorganized person and that this whole effort must definitely be discouraged. It didn't work. In fact, Rockefeller, Schmidt, and Whitney just laughed about it."

That was Johnston's first brush with Van Dyke. "I called him up and said, 'This is crazy; your kind of pressure ploy only makes me more determined to go on, and it makes you look silly.' He was furious, tenacious, and dogmatic. So the fight was on. He was determined at any cost to stop us from doing anything in New York. I told Langlois, who filled me in on the history of the troubles between the Cinémathèque and MOMA: he swept us into his universe of passion and paranoia. But it wasn't just paranoia; a lot of it was true. We used to laugh at him, but we soon learned better."

Meanwhile, the Ford Foundation had definitively dropped their support for The Eye. But Johnston was well known in New York cultural circles, and he knew Richard Clurman, an executive at Time-Life. After the death of Morton Baum, chairman of the board of the City Center, Clurman had taken over Baum's place and was trying to revitalize the City Center. In 1970 he asked Johnston to join the new City Center board and suggested he bring The Eye project to City Center, perhaps to be the nucleus for a film department there.

Langlois had no objections to this change of plan; indeed, I believe that the idea of having The Eye on Fifty-fifth Street (only two blocks from the Museum of Modern Art) rather tickled him. Clurman told Langlois and Johnston that there was a lot of unused space in the basement of the former Mecca Temple on Fifty-fifth Street, the home of City Center, and when Langlois and Johnston went to see it, accompanied by Norman Singer of the City Center, Langlois was enchanted. He liked the idea of being underground (in both senses of the word), and he thought it had the kind of proletarian, Bohemian feeling of the Left Bank in Paris. Not too fancy, and with a lot of life in the neighborhood. He was also attracted by the idea of creating something where there had been nothing before.

So Johnston, and Eugene Stavis, who had begun to work for Johnston in 1969 on the Eye project, chose the architectural firm of Oppenheimer and Brady to draw up plans. Its brief was to create three small theaters and a small exhibition space. Gradually, the idea of The Eye was metamorphosed into something that would be called the City Center Cinematheque.

But all this took time, and Langlois was not a patient man. So when Henry Geldzahler, then head of the Metropolitan Museum's Department of Twentieth Century Art, and George Tresher, the in-house director for the Met's hundredth anniversary program for the year 1970, suggested to Johnston that Langlois put on a film program that summer, Langlois jumped at the chance. Stavis, who had previously run a film society at Boston University and worked for Contemporary Films and Janus Films, began to work full time assisting him.

Meanwhile, Johnston had left Jock Whitney and moved to the Children's Television Workshop. He started to put together a committee to work on the City Center Cinematheque project: Nell Cox, Robert Redford, Joan Ganz Cooney, Milton Glaser, Adolph Green, Henry Geldzahler, and others. There were no objections from Clurman and City Center to the Metropolitan Museum project: indeed City Center felt that it ought to work with the Metropolitan whenever possible, and a kind of contractual deal for the Cinematheque was set up. The Met gave them the space—the Grace Rainey Rogers auditorium—and took care of the publicity. City Center did the rest. At that point there were no overt larger ambitions, but the Met, City Center, Langlois, and Johnston all thought of the series as a trial balloon. The Met show worked out quite well. Langlois, contrary to dire predictions, did deliver the prints, and thus proved himself to the Met. (Only two films failed to arrive, and one of those had been lost in transit.) On the other hand, the Metropolitan series was not the popular success that Langlois, Johnston, and Stavis had expected. There were several reasons for this. The show was held at a bad time—between July 29 and September 3—and the Met is not easy to get to at night. New York audiences were not yet ready, either, to see foreign films without subtitles. And the program was too ambitious. It was divided into eleven series, and one had to buy a ticket for a whole series. The price was not high—fifteen dollars for ten films—but Langlois, unwisely, I think, mixed both old and new films in most of the series, and this probably kept many people from buying a series ticket. True, some of the series were homogeneous, like "The American Western Saga" (Buster Keaton in *Go West*, James Cruze's *The Covered Wagon*, Raoul Walsh's *The Big Trail*, Maurice Tourneur's *Last of the Mohicans*, and John Ford's *Three Bad Men*). But others, like "Series Five: Individualists," which featured two films by Cecil B. De Mille, two by Rouben Mamoulian, *Birth of a Nation*, a tribute to Darryl F. Zanuck, and Roberto Rossellini's film *The Acts of the Apostles*, were too eclectic to bring a large audience. Then, too, half the shows began at 6 p.m., which is a little early for many people in New York, especially on hot days. And projection was not of the highest standards.

Predictably, the Museum of Modern Art was upset. As early as February 1970, when the news of the series first got about, some people thought that it was a squeeze play directed against the museum's film department and the New York Film Festival by the Metropolitan and City Center.

Of course, the New York festival, which ran for only two

A PASSION FOR FILMS

weeks, had less to worry about than did the Museum of Modern Art. The museum people were frightened that Langlois's summer program at the Met might continue and eventually cut into their audience and their supply of films. I myself was kept in the dark by Langlois for some time; he told me only that he was bringing off a fantastic "coup" in New York. He played fair with the New York Film Festival—at Cannes that year he said he would not take any new film for the Met show that the festival wanted to program.

Indeed, the 1970 festival featured one of the largest contributions ever made by Langlois and the Cinémathèque. He lent us his montage film (previously shown at Cannes) consisting of extracts from French films from Lumière, Méliès, Zecca, and the whole silent school of French filmmaking: it ran for over two hours, and we made a full afternoon of it by also showing *Langlois*, a film by Eila Hershon and Roberto Guerra, which featured interviews with Langlois as well as Jeanne Moreau, Lillian Gish, Ingrid Bergman, Simone Signoret, Catherine Deneuve, François Truffaut, and Viva.

Also, as part of a special events program, he offered us eleven films in a brief survey entitled "Film and Color." (Martin Scorsese says that Langlois was the first to warn him about the deterioration of color film when they met at that 1970 program, when Scorsese's *Street Scenes 1970* was part of the main festival). There were hand-painted films from the early days, tinted and toned silent films (including a French-tinted print of *The Cabinet of Dr. Caligari* that was so badly buckled we could not get it through the projectors) and prewar color (Lang's *Return of Frank James* and *Western Union*) which proved, when seen in nitrate prints, to be as beautiful as Langlois had predicted.

Somehow, with all he was doing, Langlois took time to help found the Pacific Film Archive in Berkeley, California. Sheldon Renan had begun planning the archive (part of the

University of California) in 1967, but no existing film institutions, museums, or archives were willing to help or even offer advice. Then in 1968 Simone Swann, an associate of John de Menil, brought Renan and Langlois together. Langlois, as usual, made the quick decision: yes, he trusted Renan, he liked him. (It has been suggested that Langlois was also eager to show up the Museum of Modern Art, which had refused any help until the archive had a legal existence.) "All we had," says Renan, "was a piece of paper with a statement of goals, which we showed to Langlois. He believed the archive would happen. And he began to help make it happen. He flew to Berkeley to help us plan. He counseled us, introduced us to directors and to people who would later give us grants. And he sent us films, wonderful films—*L'Age d'Or*, *La Chienne*, unknown works by Méliès—that had never been seen in Berkeley. Once Henri recognized the archive as an archive, we *became* an archive, a *cinémathèque* with credentials. It gave us an enormous head start. I cannot tell you how important Langlois's support was, how much time it saved during those years when all we had were a few films in an office, a file drawer, a borrowed auditorium, and some goals on a piece of paper."

When the university authorities asked the Cinémathèque for a written agreement—to legalize the situation—Langlois refused to sign anything but an agreement between himself and Sheldon Renan. He wouldn't deal with institutions, only with people. As a result, both Sheldon Renan and his successor Tom Luddy had a few skirmishes with the university; but the Pacific Film Archive flourishes.

After the Met show, Langlois, Johnston, and Stavis thought they were all set to go ahead with the plans for the basement of City Center. But then City Center had second thoughts—which they did not reveal immediately to Langlois. There was an idea of financing the whole of their activity by a real-estate operation: they would tear down the building and build a skyscraper on the site.

During this time when the City Center's thinking was in a state of flux, a new prospect appeared. Robert Brannigan, then on the staff of City Center, proposed that the ever-growing problems of the Vivian Beaumont Theater at Lincoln Center (where he had been technical director) might be solved by having City Center take over the building. The City of New York, it was said, would pay five million dollars for a renovation of the Beaumont, Lincoln Center would transfer its ownership to City Center for one dollar a year, on condition that City Center would then become responsible for the Beaumont.

Brannigan arranged meetings between Clurman and John Mazzola, president of Lincoln Center, and with Tom Johnston and Gene Stavis. Neither Johnston nor Stavis was enchanted with the idea: to them, it represented "gold-plated" culture as well as a built-in "white-elephant" overhead. Clurman argued that they could "democratize" the building, and since Johnston had agreed to join City Center, he felt obliged to consider the idea.

Langlois knew nothing of this development. In fact, he left for New York in the spring of 1970 firmly believing that work had begun on the basement of the Fifty-fifth Street theater. Apparently, Brannigan's suggestion for the Beaumont had come the very day before that reconstruction was to begin. Langlois was not told of the possible change because, apparently, it was "too delicate" to discuss on the phone. When he was taken to see the Beaumont, he was horrified. "A necropolis," he kept saying. "It's a necropolis."

Lincoln Center was under great pressure to reduce the

Beaumont's deficit. Johnston and Stavis were not overly enchanted with the idea of using the Beaumont, but Clurman was under pressure from Lincoln Center, and since he was not an unambitious man, he was captivated by the idea of being able to get Lincoln Center out of its predicament and also to acquire a new building for the City Center.

Contrary to what was said at the time, there was never any plan to throw legitimate theater out of the building. The idea that architects Oppenheimer and Brady came up with was simply to transfer bodily the two-hundred-seat Forum Theater (now the Mitzi E. Newhouse Theater) from its place in the basement to the backstage area of the Beaumont. This was feasible because the backstage area had been built on a large enough scale to house a dozen sets (for the repertory company that never existed as such).

The basement would then have been transformed into a film center. There was never any plan to take over the main theater. Offices would be built in the 106-foot-high backstage area which had been designed for a cyclorama (which had turned out to be inoperable). The lobby, however, would have had to be redesigned, and the main theater would have been used for film whenever the theater was normally "dark."

In view of the battle that soon arose, it is ironic that Langlois himself was never convinced that the Beaumont was a good place for a Cinematheque operation. It was the opposite of everything he had wanted—too chic, too physically inconvenient, and too intimidating. But Langlois realized that the Fifty-fifth Street basement plan was no longer possible, and agreed, with deep misgivings, to the new project.

No sooner had Langlois accepted the idea than the battle to "save the Beaumont" began. It was begun by Dore Schary, former film producer and at that time Commissioner of Parks and Recreation for New York City; he started a petition (signed by luminaries like Helen Hayes and Eva Le Gallienne) to save the Beaumont from film. There were hearings before the City Council and great public debate. Although it was not clear at the time, the chief objection now seems to have been to moving the Forum Theater: the designer of the theater, Jo Mielziner, referred to the Cinematheque/City Center people as the "Seizers of the Forum." And in fact, most New Yorkers erroneously believed that the legitimate theater was to be thrown out of the Beaumont.

It might all have worked out nonetheless, except that at a crucial City Council meeting Jules Irving did an apparent volte-face and claimed that the Beaumont company was in great shape and didn't need money from anyone. It has been suggested that he did this because he had already received a promise of money from Mitzi Newhouse—money which eventually did come, bringing about the change in name from the Forum Theater to the Mitzi E. Newhouse Theater. And Dore Schary's committee claimed it had assurances of money from an unnamed group of people. Ironically, theater producer Joseph Papp supported the Schary committee's views—only to discover for himself several years later just how unviable a theater the Beaumont was. By the end of 1971, the Beaumont plan for the City Center Cinematheque was dead. Langlois was not too upset—although the violence of the opposition did shock him. But now a new site had to be found.

11

The Museum of the Cinema

L anglois did not spend all his time in New York during 1970 and 1971, although some people in Paris said rather bitterly that his "weekends in New York" had become "weekends in Paris" instead. Since he had taken the plunge into teaching in Montreal, and since the need for money for the Cinémathèque was still pressing, he accepted Jean Rouch's invitation to teach a film course at a division of the University of Paris in Nanterre. It paid well, and Langlois taught there for three years. He was, Rouch told me, outraged when he got a tax claim. He seemed to think that, since it was the government who was paying him to teach at Nanterre, they had no right to ask him to pay taxes. Mary Meerson, in fact, thought the university ought to pay his income tax for him. The only way Rouch was able to explain the situation was by analogy: "Mary," he said, "it's like being invited to dinner at someone's house and then expecting them to pay your taxi fare." That she seemed to understand. Nonetheless, Langlois lost the tax form, and when they caught up with him five years later he had to pay both the tax and a whopping fine.

I went out to suburban Nanterre to hear his inaugural lecture. In spite of Godard's La Chinoise, in spite of all the documentary footage I had seen, nothing had prepared me for the horror of Nanterre. Approaching it by car, you see a treeless plain (it used to be well forested, but the trees were cut down when the university was built) and bleak, unfinished concrete buildings, already flecked with dirt, already peeling. Godard's fury against what the government had done to the suburbs came back with a shudder: what he had said was true. That day the students were demonstrating against the increase in tuition and dormitory rents, the lack of space, the unfinished library. Actually, once there, one could imagine them protesting about the place itself. Not a café for miles, no place to congregate, just grayness as far as one could see.

The lecture was brilliant—so much so that after it was over a young man approached Langlois to invite him to give a course at Vincennes, another division of the University of Paris. "Ah, non!" said Langlois. "I've got too much to do at the Cinémathèque." One understood the enthusiasm of the man from Vincennes: the lecture was about the films of Lumière; not a subject to excite students, one would have thought, but Langlois was able to communicate his enthusiasm, to make them see the films, and even to follow him through a tangled exposition of the insoluble problem of who actually invented the cinema. In summing up, he said that just as America existed before Columbus, so the cinema existed before any of its inventors, a sort of Platonic idea that one would not imagine appealing to the radical students of Nanterre.

But they took it all in; as the administrative assistant said to me (thus shedding light on what usually went on), "It's wonderful! They didn't talk during his lecture, not even during the film clips."

For Langlois, the opening of the Museum of the Cinema in June 1972 was the crowning achievement of his career, a long-cherished dream come true. The idea had come to him before the war, when he began to collect posters, models, sketches, a Méliès camera, "more or less anything I could lay my hands on." Indeed, in the first statutes of the Cinémathèque, signed in 1936, Article Two included a provision, as an essential part of the enterprise, for the conservation of documents, photographs, articles, books, manuscripts, maquettes of decor, musical scores, etc. It was only after the war, however, that the idea quickened into life: the avenue de Messine in 1949 was the prefiguration in miniature of the museum.

For over thirty years, aided by the indefatigable Lotte Eisner, Langlois collected whatever he could: sometimes he bought things at auction, other things were given to him, and occasionally, as Derek Prouse told me, he would simply take things. "Anything to do with the cinema was sacred to Langlois. When he and Lotte came to see me in my flat, they were not above going through my shelves and drawers when I was in the kitchen making coffee. Once they found a script that Leopoldo Torre Nilsson, the Argentine director, had left, and before I knew it they had wrapped it up and said, 'Darling, you don't mind if we take this, do you?' "

The idea of a real museum was very important to him: for a decade before the museum opened, the Chaillot theater was officially called the Museum of the Cinema. The screenings were, for Langlois, part of what Malraux would have called the "Museum without Walls." And I believe he was piqued by the remark in the Heilbronner Report that the museum had only "a theoretical existence." Langlois was determined, in spite of financial difficulties, that one day he would have a real museum; the Musée d'Art Moderne show in 1955, the Méliès show of 1962, and the Hôtel Martinez show at Cannes were, however successful, however satisfying, no substitute for a permanent museum that would give to the cinema the status of the other arts.

Not everyone shared Langlois's view. François Truffaut, for example, felt that Langlois should have reopened the Cinémathèque library (which had been in packing cases, unavailable, since the departure from the avenue de Messine in 1955) instead. Hundreds of millions of francs were swallowed up by the museum. In an interview in *American Film*, Truffaut said:

> If the Cinémathèque had unlimited funds at its disposal, a museum might find its proper place there. Personally I see little value in displaying a dress worn by Greta Garbo. The Cinémathèque's major function must be the preservation of films, especially nitrate-based prints. . . . And the money spent on the museum would have enabled at least 500 nitrate prints to have been copied on safety stock.[1]

But Truffaut's objections went deeper. Later he told me: "Everyone in Langlois's entourage flattered him, saying things like 'Only Henri could put this photo of Griffith next to that

The Museum of the Cinema

one of Asta Nielsen.' I don't believe in that. You thumbtack a still, and that's that. Putting a Garbo costume next to the skull from *Psycho* was a gimmick for tourists. Who cares about seeing a lot of old projectors? Both the preservation of films and the adventurousness of the programming of Chaillot in its early days were sacrificed to the museum. It just wasn't worth it."

For Georges Goldfayn, who had worked with Langlois in the sixties, the museum was a kind of King Tut's tomb. Langlois sacrificed everything to it because he wanted to leave something permanent behind—a pyramid. And the programs suffered: money for the museum became all-important, so that the films were chosen to bring the largest possible audiences. "He spent all his time at Chaillot, and the programming was done on the phone to the Courcelles offices."

Jean Riboud confirms that it was indeed the box-office receipts that largely helped finance the museum. Financially, it was insane to try to create the museum then. But Langlois felt that his time was running out. He got the space initially by pretending it was only for a temporary exhibition, hoping that people who saw the "exhibition" would be so impressed that he could get the locale for keeps. And so they were. But there was no real state aid; money from the box office was not enough, and more had to be raised from private sources. Ultimately, the museum was built on debt: the staff wasn't paid on time, and Langlois owed money to the Social Security service. It was not, as his enemies claimed, financial disorder or underhand dealings that landed the Cinémathèque with enormous debts: it was simply, says Riboud, that the available money went to the museum.

Yet many people felt that the museum was worth it. The accusation that Langlois was a mere fetishist (Why bother collecting sketches, costumes, etc.? All that counts is the

A PASSION FOR FILMS

films.) was answered by director Karel Reisz: "If I was doing research into the films of, say, William Wyler, I think it would be very helpful to see the set designs, so that I could compare the original with what turned up on the screen. Every little bit helps, you know. All that stuff is very intriguing." Jean Rouch, also, disagrees with Truffaut and Goldfayn: for him, the museum is a work of genius, "a *mise en scène* of the great *metteurs en scène*." Langlois planned the museum in the same way he planned programs: by putting a film with Harry Langdon alongside one by Dziga Vertov, he would create a montage, even if he didn't have the films. "I remember," says Rouch, "Langlois once asked me whether I thought it would be a good idea to program Man Ray's *L'Étoile de Mer* with Nicholas Ray's *Rebel Without a Cause*. I said I did, and then Langlois told me that neither film was available at that moment, but he was putting them into the mimeographed program nonetheless. 'In one hundred years,' he said, 'people will see that the two films were programmed together, and then they'll do it, and they'll be the ones to see the connection. They'll see what we're not able to see or show now.' "

Langlois's museum was a three-dimensional film, *his* history of the cinema. Or, as David Robinson wrote:

Langlois portrays film history like a painter, using the resources of the Cinémathèque's collections (the sixty rooms in the museum—500 feet long—can scarcely house one-tenth of the collection) to create his own sort of collage. His exhibitions are not formal instructional displays with neat dates and labels; they work through unexpected but meaningful juxtapositions of disparate material. . . . All these artifacts are tangible links, establishing a continuity between the two-dimensional image and real life, bridges between reality and dream, between the maker and the object, witnesses of the act of creation.[2]

The Museum of the Cinema

A naive visitor might think that the museum was just made up as it went along—for example, there doesn't seem to be enough room for recent developments. Everything from the Neo-Realists to the present, including holograms, is compressed into the last three rooms, as if Langlois had suddenly run out of space. But it's not because Langlois hadn't planned the museum carefully. Sallie Blumenthal (former administrative director of the New York Film Festival and, from 1971, Langlois's unofficial, unpaid American representative) has written about her visit with her husband to the Palais de Chaillot in September 1971—almost a year before the show opened. Langlois escorted them.

> The space was huge, long and narrow, covering the entire floor of the east wing of the Palais de Chaillot. As he guided us around the museum, talking and gesticulating for an hour and a half, he pointed out costumes and sets, scripts, posters, props, projectors, cameras, puppets, projection machines, and much more, vividly evoking the entire history of the cinema, as well as its antecedents and its relationships to the other arts. It was a unique experience—unique because Langlois communicated so much to us, and because in fact the space was empty—entirely bare![3]

If recent film history is compressed into three rooms, it is because Langlois felt that what had come before was more important to show now: the films of the postwar period were sufficiently fresh in everyone's minds so as not to need as much loving evocation. Then, too, the exhibition which stands today was not meant to be permanent. It was, in Langlois's mind, only the beginning of an evolving display which he intended to revise and adapt through the years. Some objects—like Edison's 1889 strip Kinetograph—were only lent for two months. It was the only one in existence, and the Edison National Historical Site in New Jersey lent it on condition that it be brought over and taken back, in a special crate, by one of their staff. Unfortunately, although a catalog was written, there was never enough money to print it. Nor were there any labels on the exhibits. When I asked Langlois why, he said, "Haven't you noticed people going through art museums? They come into a room, see a picture, walk over to read the label, discover who the picture is by and what its title is, and then move on. They have read; they know. I don't want that sort of thing in my museum. I want people to look at everything, really look, and if there are no labels then they have to try to figure out what the object or photograph is. That is the difference between an illustrated book with its captions and a museum: it's not important that people should know exactly what still came from which film; the whole museum has been planned as an almost autonomous living history of the cinema. What's important is not to know that here we have a picture of Lillian Gish but rather—since the museum is in chronological order—what a star of the cinema looked like at a given time."*

The museum cost four million francs; it would have cost twenty million if it had been planned and constructed by the state. Langlois got some of the money from business and industrial sources: here Jean Riboud of the Schlumberger company was the greatest help. But Langlois also persuaded a large electrical appliance firm to donate the lighting fixtures. The showcases were sold to him at cost. And for months he and his small staff worked eighty-hour weeks: painting, papering, covering the walls with cloth.

The space the museum occupies was formerly that of the

---

*And yet the Martinez show *had* had labels; maybe the Cannes Festival had insisted.

The Museum of the Cinema

Musée National des Arts et Traditions Populaires, which moved out in the late sixties. This move had been in the cards for a long time and was one of the reasons why Langlois and Malraux both wanted the Cinémathèque screening room where it was—at the end of the huge arc of the east wing of the Palais de Chaillot. The museum was meant to be a prologue to the screenings.

Typically, the museum was finished only just before it was due to open. Sallie Blumenthal remembers arriving at Charles de Gaulle Airport the night before the museum was to be inaugurated. She was driven directly to Chaillot, where she arrived at half past ten. There was Langlois, padding around in his stocking feet, half dead with fatigue (he had been without sleep for forty-eight hours), and in the middle of the floor a pathetic-looking pair of moccasins (his). They embraced, and he went back to work. From time to time, worn-out but exhilarated, he would come back to talk to her. Mrs. Blumenthal left at 4 a.m., but he stayed on. She arrived at ten the next morning to find him still at work, frantic because there was no one to sew up a seam in Giulietta Masina's costume from *La Strada*. "Can you sew?" he asked Sallie. When she said she could, a needle and thread were found, and she sat down on the steps and sewed away. No sooner had she finished than he snatched the costume from her hands and, stopping only to adjust Esther Williams's bathing suit, immediately attached the Masina costume to the wall. All the while, a dozen people were waiting around for him to tell them what to do next.

It was a tricky space, for although it was five hundred feet long, it was only thirty feet wide, and so could not easily be divided into rooms. Instead, Langlois made a kind of labyrinth: little partitions made one move from left to right and back again, and there were dead-end pockets.

Perhaps the most spectacular attraction was the reconstruction of a set from *The Cabinet of Dr. Caligari*, done by Hermann Warm, then eighty-two, who was one of the original team of designers for that film. This coup was arranged by Lotte Eisner. Langlois said that Eisner was responsible for two thirds of the museum, but she would demur, claiming only to be the one who actually laid her hands on the materials: it was he who arranged them and made them into what they became. For example, as one walks into the *Caligari* set (it is life-size), one sees through the wings a blowup of a still from Lubitsch's *Madame Dubarry* (United States title: *Passion*), made at about the same time as *Caligari*. It doesn't belong there, in a sense, but seeing it tells you more about the coexistence of various styles than volumes of film history—if, of course, you can recognize it without a label. And if Vivien Leigh's ball gown from *Gone With the Wind* has gone gray with age, seeing it casually draped near Esther Williams's pearl bathing suit and not too far from Chanel's costume for Delphine Seyrig in *Last Year at Marienbad* prompts fruitful musings about the relationship between history and the cinema, between cinema and fashion.

Langlois treated each period of film history differently: the Italian neorealist epoch is brilliantly summed up in one room with huge blowups of shots from *Bicycle Thief*, *Open City*, and *La Strada*. Perhaps most extraordinary was the great charm of so many of the artifacts. Méliès's painted backdrops, and his maquettes, are works of art in themselves. The robot from Fritz Lang's *Metropolis*, the tiny houses which form the set by Lazare Meerson for René Clair's *Under the Roofs of Paris*, turn out to be enchanting in their own right. Nor is Art with a capital A absent: there are drawings by Fernand Léger as well as the original wood sculpture he made for his film *Le Ballet Mécanique*. There are Tom Mix's cowboy suits, the shrunken head from *Psycho*, donated by Hitchcock, the crown from

Kurosawa's *Throne of Blood*. Each in itself might have been trivial, but together they form an atmosphere unmatched anywhere. As you wander from space to space, the history of the cinema unfolds before your astonished eyes.

Because the museum depends on significant juxtaposition, it is useless to list the objects, remarkable as many of them are (Griffith scripts, early cameras and projectors, Bessie Love's dress from *The Broadway Melody*, drawings by Eisenstein, Russian constructivist posters, Valentino's robe from *The Sheik*, costumes designed by Kurosawa). If the museum was an indulgence of Langlois's, as some claim, or "a fine testimony to the futility of trying to preserve a transient art," as Joseph Losey maintains, surely Langlois after his years of collecting, preserving, and showing films had earned the right to a little self-indulgence.

Unfortunately, only a few months after the museum was opened, it had to be temporarily closed. Lotte Eisner had warned, "Henri, you have left too many things out in the open. They will be touched, damaged, stolen. You must put plate glass over them." But he didn't—or couldn't—and James Dean's leather jacket was stolen, as well as Marilyn Monroe's dress from *The Seven Year Itch*. These thefts bothered Langlois less than one would have imagined. As he said to Rouch, "It doesn't matter that someone has stolen a Marilyn Monroe costume: don't tell Mary, but I've got five more, and even if all of them were stolen, I'd get Pierre Cardin to do me a new one. The museum is a museum of the imaginary: if someone steals Marilyn's dress, that proves they loved it and her, so one has only to foresee such things and have extra copies. This is a living museum." Nevertheless, since there was no money for the large number of guards that the labyrinthine plan necessitated, when the museum reopened, it was for conducted groups only.

Soon after the museum closed, Langlois lost the theater on the rue d'Ulm. The Musée Pédagogique, which had welcomed Langlois in 1956, said it needed the auditorium. So in 1973 it threw the Cinémathèque out. Some felt that the institute was yielding to pressure from the art houses of the Latin Quarter; when Langlois was programming with both eyes on the box office, he showed some films that were already scheduled by the art houses, and this was perhaps unfair competition (especially as his seat prices were much lower).

The loss of the rue d'Ulm theater was somewhat compensated for by a small theater at the end of the labyrinth of the museum. So by October 1973, the Cinémathèque was back to showing seven films a day—four, and sometimes five, in the big theater in Chaillot, and three in the small screening room of the museum, with its backless chairs.

All this activity would have been more than enough for any one man to undertake. But during this time Langlois never lost sight of his American projects. The fifty thousand dollars paid him as consultant to the American/City Center Cinematheque went—like all the money he earned abroad, or at Nanterre—straight into the coffers of the Cinémathèque. City Center, too, paid for part of the expenses of the museum, so there could be no question of abandoning the New York project. When the American Cinematheque was finally set up, then Langlois would go back to paying more attention to programming, to conservation, to collection; then, and only then, could he rest. His health had deteriorated; he continued to suffer from gout, high blood pressure, and overwhelming fatigue. But meanwhile, he had to keep going as best he could on two continents, fighting two sets of battles.

12

Underneath the Arches

G ene Stavis and his colleague Kathy St. John (former executive secretary to Mayor John V. Lindsay) spent six months in 1972 looking for another site for the City Center Cinematheque. They were offered disused or moribund movie theaters—the Fillmore East, the Bleecker Street Cinema, the New Yorker. But Stavis and St. John were after a more flexible space. The original idea had been two or three screening rooms with access to the Cinémathèque Française collection (and others), running fourteen hours a day; it would have been like a library where a great number of films would be shown, "good" and "bad": one would be able to see almost everything. In addition to this, Langlois later had urged them to aim for enough space for a museum.

Opposition to the implantation of a *cinémathèque* in New York continued. There were two distinct objections. First, that such an organization would diminish the audiences of the Museum of Modern Art film department. To this objection Johnston replied that both Willard Van Dyke of the museum and Martin E. Segal, then president of the Film Society of Lincoln Center, were wrong: "They thought that only a few people should control film in New York . . . but there are many audiences in New York." On this point he may well have been right. The second objection was raised by Segal; he maintained that there was a limited "pie" of money available for funding film in New York, that it was difficult enough for the Museum of Modern Art's film department to survive without another organization drawing some of that money away. Johnston denied this in 1972; but perhaps Segal, because of his financial connections and acumen, knew or sensed that money was about to become tight, and the events of 1973 (the oil crisis, for example) proved him right.

Meanwhile, the search for a location went on. Stavis and St. John got a list of empty spaces owned by the city, and investigated all of them, until they came across a space under the Queensborough Bridge, on First Avenue between Fifty-ninth and Sixtieth streets. They told Johnston about it; he passed the news to Jacquelin Robertson, head of the City Planning Commission, and his partner Richard Bernstein. Langlois was taken to see it, and Sallie Blumenthal reports, "I never saw his eyes light up more than when he walked into that space. 'It's like a cathedral,' he said." And it had no connection with establishment culture.

Johnston, too, was enthusiastic, as was his friend the architect I. M. Pei. Johnston got a $100,000 planning grant from the Ford Foundation, and with Pei offering to draw up the plans at cost, they started on the engineering blueprints. They also had to concern themselves with weatherproofing the roof (the roadbed of the bridge). Graphic designer Milton Glaser did their presentation gratis. Richard Clurman of City Center was excited about the idea, as was the Astor Foundation. But it took six months of battling with the Community Board to get planning permission for the fantastic scheme.

The project was to use the space under the vaulted arches supporting the bridge. This had been an open market after the bridge was built in 1909; in 1918 a fountain was added. A year later, the area was glassed in, and the market continued until the mid-1930s. Since then the space had been used only for municipal storage: signs, police barricades, etc. Pei's plan was to restore and protect the grandeur of the original Guastavino tile vaulting which formed the cathedral-like structure. Because the site followed the slope of the land toward the East River, it varied in height between thirty and sixty feet from west to east. This would make ramps and multilevel spaces an attractive and natural way to accommodate varied uses. Most of the interior would have been clearly visible through new glass in the handsome exterior arches: the intention was a planned aesthetic counterpoint with the almost medieval quality of the old structure. Outside, the parking lot was to be transformed into a public park maintained by the Cinematheque. There was to be a 500-seat theater under a dome outside the structure, and two interior auditoriums (one with 250 seats, the other with 150), as well as a 50-seat screening room for scholars and staff members. Furthermore, there was to be 25,000 square feet of space for exhibitions on film art and history. There would also be a restaurant, a bookstore, facilities for conferences and for research, offices, open spaces for visitors, and a flower market. Films were to be shown from morning to midnight, and they were expected to draw from three to five thousand people daily.

The project was kept quiet for as long as possible, but somehow the story was leaked to the *New York Times* and appeared on April 13, 1973. This was unfortunate because the American Cinematheque (as it was now officially called) did not yet have any funding. Johnston had spoken to the Astor Foundation, which was interested in parts of the project—the landscaping and the flower market, but not in the film part. The project was estimated to cost ten million dollars.

When the story appeared in the *New York Times*, Ada Louise Huxtable was enthusiastic. "The vaulted space," as she put it, "would make a romantic interior that could not be duplicated today. And the style of the architect's additions," she wrote, "was strikingly contemporary."[1] But a project costing such an enormous amount of money only increased the opposition. Van Dyke went on record as saying, "With every cultural institution in New York facing financial problems, it seems to me that another place to show classic motion pictures should have a very low priority for funding."[2]

Ironically, by the time the plans were announced the project was already doomed: the recession had begun, and the Astor and Ford foundations started to withdraw. City Center itself was retrenching: they cut support for several ballet companies, and there was no longer any way for them to continue their annual retainer of fifty thousand dollars to Langlois and the Cinémathèque Française.

But Johnston and Stavis didn't stop trying. Stavis, interviewed by the *Times* on March 10, 1974, reported that fundraising was proceeding in a "leisurely but energetic" way— surely a contradiction in terms if not something of a smoke screen. But little progress was actually being made. They had needed four million to start with, which in 1972 hadn't seemed too difficult to raise, but then money got tight. "The portfolio of the Ford Foundation," says Johnston, "dropped from six to four billion dollars." And the idea seemed less important to everyone: institutions such as the Metropolitan Opera and the Metropolitan Museum had to be saved before anyone would consider a new project. Still, Johnston hoped that the economic situation might improve; he tried other avenues, other approaches, and he kept his "hold" on the site, with a one-dollar lease from the city.

Langlois, too, was optimistic: it seemed impossible to him that such a wonderful project could not find funding in such a rich city as New York. But his friend and business adviser, Jean Riboud, was convinced that the project was doomed the moment City Center suspended its payments to Langlois in April. At that point Langlois could have pulled out of the operation, but he was determined to persevere. He suggested to Riboud that they sue the City Center, but Riboud explained that even if they won, they wouldn't get any money, because there was none. The City of New York itself was close to bankruptcy, and a lawsuit would be throwing money away on lawyers and court costs. Langlois and Meerson couldn't believe that City Center and the municipality didn't have the money. And they wouldn't give up: Langlois, says Riboud, was full of hopes and dreams, and there was always someone in New York to tell him that it was all going to happen— tomorrow, next week, next month. And as long as there was someone to pay for his trips to New York and his hotel room (at his favorite hotel, the Salisbury, almost opposite the Russian Tea Room, and next to his beloved Greek restaurant, Piraeus My Love), he was ready to take off for New York at a moment's notice.

Even after the American Cinematheque was obliged to separate itself from the City Center in the winter of 1975–76, there was still the hope that the Metropolitan Museum would help. Indeed, a three-year contract with the Met was drawn up with a view to establishing a film department there. But Langlois was not satisfied with some of the conditions in the three-way contract between the Met, the American Cinematheque, and the Cinémathèque Française, and he never did sign it.

L anglois still had enough energy to make 1974 another *annus mirabilis* for the Cinémathèque. On March 2 he pulled off what was to be perhaps the most spectacular event in its history. At the Porte Maillot, the western gate of Paris, on the far side of the Arc de Triomphe, there had been built, as part of the work involved in the new "beltway" around Paris, an enormous convention center—the Palais des Congrès. The palace, however, being new and on the edge of town, needed to be spectacularly launched in order to make its presence known and felt. Georges Cravenne, impresario/press agent, who is the Parisian specialist in premieres and launchings, had the brilliant idea of offering the palace to the Cinémathèque for a day, and enough money for Langlois to do whatever he wanted.

Langlois decided to offer a nonstop day of films, from 10 in the morning to 10:30 at night. He would show films not only from his own collection but from the film libraries of thirty-five countries—as well as the latest works of budding filmmakers. In fact, he was to make use of no fewer than twenty improvised theaters within the vast space of the palace. The main hall (3,700 seats) was to be devoted to a nonstop montage—by Langlois—of excerpts of films about Paris: "Paris through the cinema, from Lumière to our time." The next largest hall, 750 seats, was to be devoted to masterpieces of documentary cinema since 1928. The 380-seat hall was for films about World War II, including the "Why We Fight" series of documentaries made by Frank Capra for the American army. In the 360-seat hall young filmmakers could bring their latest 16 mm efforts, to be shown without any process of selection, except for the obvious one of "first come, first served." There were sixteen other rooms, with seating capacities ranging from 70 to 200 seats, in which foreign archives could show their treasures.

There was a certain amount of confusion as to what was being shown where. There were dozens of "hostesses," but since they were employees of the Palais des Congrès, they were not well informed about the film programs. Finally, a loudspeaker system was put into use, with announcements—as in an airport—like "It is now 6 p.m. The Soviet theater is full. There is only standing room for 'Why We Fight.' But there are seats available for Canada, Algeria, and India."

Naturally, such an ambitious—not to say insane—project was not carried out without a few slip-ups. A sizable audience was at the Porte Maillot by 10 o'clock, but the program in the large hall didn't begin until 10:30, with some extraordinary views of turn-of-the-century Paris by the Lumière brothers. The program, due to last twelve hours, had only got as far as Marcel Carné and the thirties by 7 p.m., so Langlois never got to Paris as seen by the New Wave.

To give some idea of the kind of people who turned out for the show, I remember that during lunch a few friends and I were talking about Renoir's *La Chienne*, from which we had just seen an extract. Suddenly an elderly lady at the next table leaned over and said she couldn't help hearing what we were saying, and she just wanted to tell us that she had personally known Janie Marèse, the star of *La Chienne*, who had been killed in a car accident just after the shooting of the film was finished—so she never got a chance to see her greatest film. The atmosphere was like that of some medieval fair. There were complaints: some people had come to see a specific film and either couldn't learn where it was being screened, or found there were no seats left, or discovered that the film was not being shown at all. But we all felt privileged to be participating in a once-in-a-lifetime experience. Even today, some of the people who were there talk about it as one of the most extraordinary events they have ever attended.

The day was placed under the patronage of Blanche Sweet, one of D. W. Griffith's actresses, and still very much interested not only in the cinema of her day but in later films as well. And Langlois? He wasn't much in evidence; he spent most of his time in the projection room where the history-of-Paris program was going on. Not altogether smoothly: apparently the "montage" was not fully prepared in advance, so Langlois spent his time grabbing reels of film and handing them to the projectionists, saying, "Put that on now." There were interruptions, and some films were not in chronological order. But this was not meant to be a scientific study of Paris: Langlois took a much more impressionistic approach.

Some people wandered from theater to theater; others preferred to stay put. But what pleased Langlois most about this day was that the audience was composed not only of the regulars, but of people who had never been to the Cinémathèque. The screenings were free, they had received a lot of publicity, and the crowd was enormous, growing gradually as Saturday wore on. Langlois hoped that many of the people there would now find their way to regular Cinémathèque screenings. But I think it was the sheer challenge of the operation that excited him most; this was something no one had ever done before. It made up for a lot of the day-to-day worries and heartaches of running the Cinémathèque and the frustrations involved with New York.

Unfortunately, I wasn't able to stay through the evening, for Langlois dragged me to a dinner at the Club Méditerranée Hotel for the representatives of the archives whose films had been lent for the show. That, too, was a kind of triumph for him: it showed to the world that he could get films from almost everywhere, even though the Cinémathèque had not been a member of FIAF for nearly fifteen years.

According to the critic of *L'Express*, more than four hundred films from over thirty-five countries were shown during those fourteen hours: this is probably an approximate figure because, unless one were actually present in all twenty theaters all day, one could not be sure that all the films announced were actually shown. But there were enough to make the day a triumph.

Three weeks later, to launch a Gloria Swanson series, the Cinémathèque gave a seventy-fifth birthday party for Miss Swanson at Chaillot, an event that once again got headlines for Langlois in most of the Paris newspapers. The French are particularly fond of Miss Swanson (and vice versa) because she made what she claims to be her best film there: *Madame Sans-Gêne*, directed by Léonce Perret, now unfortunately lost. Furthermore, she had married a Frenchman, the Marquis de La Falaise. Appearing in a slinky blue and green diagonally striped gown, Miss Swanson blew out the candles on her birthday cake. The photograph of her and the candles appeared in newspapers and magazines all over the world. The cake ceremony was followed by a montage of sequences from her best films, and many Parisians were astonished to realize that before becoming the vamp, the diva, of the twenties, she had been a Mack Sennett bathing beauty, and a very accomplished comedienne. The montage had not been prepared by

Langlois himself but by James Card of Eastman House, and it had in fact been test-run a month before in Orlando, Florida, as part of central Florida's first film festival. Card and Langlois, however, did add a few extra films for the Paris homage, including *Zaza* and *Queen Kelly*.

It was a glorious occasion, but it was costly. The Cinémathèque paid for Miss Swanson's round-trip airline ticket and her hotel. The Swanson evening was one of the examples that Langlois's adversaries cited to show how he "squandered" money. Miss Swanson could, they said, have paid her own way. They didn't realize that you cannot get stars to be present at such an occasion unless they are invited (i.e., paid for). Stars are used to being treated as stars, and Langlois knew this. Should that money have been spent on making duplicates of dissolving prints? Should it have been used to raise the low salaries of the Cinémathèque employees? Perhaps. But Langlois believed that the prestige of the Cinémathèque, and indeed of all such archives, depended on having such expensive indulgences from time to time. He valued that prestige not for himself but because most of the "expensive" visitors to Chaillot eventually paid their way, as it were, in prints left behind (or loaned for duplicating) and in objects for the museum. The publicity that it brought was important, both to encourage people to come to the Cinémathèque and to make other filmmakers and actors want to donate prints and artifacts to the collection.

In fact, were it not for the publicity that Langlois garnered with such events, it is doubtful that he would have won his Oscar, his third great event of 1974. Mary Meerson insisted that he needed a new suit especially for the occasion, and she persuaded Pierre Cardin (who had already made suits for Langlois in exchange for the occasional private screening) to make him a midnight-blue tuxedo. Langlois flatly refused to go to Cardin to be measured, so Cardin sent a man to the Cinémathèque. Langlois, however, refused to stand up. The poor tailor tried to explain that it was impossible to measure a man sitting down, but Langlois was adamant: and finally that was how he was measured.

Langlois went to Hollywood for ten days, where he was wined and dined by the foreign colony—Fritz Lang, Jean Renoir—and he also met King Vidor, Groucho Marx (who appeared in blue jeans with cane and cigar, to sit literally at Langlois's feet), Rouben Mamoulian, not to mention an afternoon *chez* Mae West.

Finally, on April 2, Langlois was presented by the Academy of Motion Picture Arts and Sciences with an honorary Oscar, given by Jack Valenti, president of the MPAA, who hailed Langlois as "the conscience of the cinema." Langlois's acceptance speech was translated by Gene Kelly: "Around 1916–1917 in France, everyone who counted, or I should say, all the really important artists in France (Picasso, Diaghilev, Proust, and Stravinsky) went crazy about the American cinema. They fell in love with it to such an extent that it uplifted the creators and makers of French films from Delluc, Renoir, and Gance way back then, all the way down to Truffaut and Godard in our time." And then, in English, Langlois added, "This is the reason I like so much the film American, and nice to meet you."

The Oscar was, as James Card wrote, "of profound importance to him—to the surprise of some who thought they knew him better." If the American Cinematheque was still not off the ground, the Oscar was at least some compensation from his beloved America. According to Card, however, the Oscar was, for his enemies, the final signal to close in for the kill. This may be an exaggeration, but many other archivists, including those at the Museum of Modern Art in New York, thought that Langlois should not have been the first of their kind to be so honored.

Not surprisingly, the programming and preservation activities of the Cinémathèque Française had gone into a decline. Langlois's energy had diminished, and there wasn't enough left to run the Chaillot theater properly. He could, of course, have delegated the work of programming, but he fired every assistant for showing "too much initiative." He said he was considering a kind of twelve-man program committee, of which I was willing to be a member, but just as he always talked about preparing for the future and never did anything about it (the number of people he told that they were to be his successor was large), so the program committee never came into being. That refusal to delegate was perhaps his greatest mistake in the last years.

But while Langlois always believed the worst was about to happen, he also thought that everything was just about to work out. He still believed the American Cinematheque would happen, and that it would save the Cinémathèque Française. And so in 1975 and 1976 he ran a kind of holding operation—the Cinémathèque Française kept going, just, but the programming was uninspired, and more often than not the film announced was not the film shown. A friend went five times to see Losey's M and each time the Fritz Lang M was shown instead. Dissatisfaction was growing, and began to be expressed publicly.

Nonetheless, Langlois did enjoy a kind of recognition from the government. Around Thanksgiving, 1976, he was invited to an official dinner at the Élysée Palace by the president of the republic, Valéry Giscard d'Estaing. Mary Meerson had gone back to Pierre Cardin to get Henri a cape and a tuxedo, and although Langlois never enjoyed such official functions, there was a kind of grim satisfaction in seeing the wheel of fortune come full circle.

Langlois's health, so cruelly tried, continued to give way: "the provinces of his body revolted." He was still winging across the Atlantic all the time, and I remember that when he introduced his print of Renoir's *Nana* at the 1976 New York Film Festival, he looked tired and discouraged. He had come to put together, for the spring of 1977, a Paris–New York show for the first American Cinematheque program since 1970 at the Metropolitan Museum, and he worked day and night in his room at the Salisbury Hotel.

He suffered several attacks of gout and bronchitis, and as he either had not remembered to bring his medicine from Paris or had used it up, he would ask Sallie Blumenthal to get prescriptions from her doctor—prescriptions based on his somewhat hazy recollection of the spelling of the ingredients of his French medicine. He also relied, for general purposes, on enormous quantities of rose-petal jelly, a Greek confection he had been brought up on in Smyrna, for which he had never lost the taste. He could spoon down a whole jar in ten minutes.

When he returned to Paris in December 1976, he embarked on a new project to make money for the Cinémathéque: it was an idea devised by Jean-Luc Godard and producer Jean-Pierre Rassam for a history of the cinema, to be released on film and video cassette. Langlois and Godard were to write and direct, and Rassam was to finance and produce it.

That same year, Langlois signed a contract with Jean-Charles Edeline for the rental of film vaults in the suburban town of Orsay. Many people considered this a mistake. First of all, Langlois signed the contract without consulting the ad-

ministrative council of the Cinémathèque. He didn't even
tell Jean Riboud about it until after he had signed. Secondly,
the rent for these vaults was not cheap. "It was," says Riboud,
"a fair price, but only if one accepts Langlois's refusal to use
the government's new vaults at Bois d'Arcy, which would
have been free." The most strongly rooted of Langlois's pho-
bias, however, the most tenacious of his fears, was that the
Centre National du Cinéma wanted to steal his films—and
therefore the idea of depositing prints in the Archives Na-
tionales du Film, which had been built by the CNC, was un-
thinkable. "I tried to explain to Henri," Riboud told me,
"that a contract could be made—just as one does, in a sense,
when one deposits one's money in a bank. That was the worst
example I could have chosen, because Henri was convinced
that banks always stole your money, and I had simply confirmed his worst suspicions. Langlois never had a bank account in his life, not even a checking account."

There was some foundation to Langlois's fears of the CNC.
"But Langlois always exaggerated, amplified, mythified.
There *is* some justification in keeping a film library separate
from the state. There are archives which have been national-
ized, and they are not the most respectful of copyrights. Further than that, I can't go; I have no proof that the CNC had
designs on the Cinémathèque's collections. Henri might have
been prepared to deposit his collection with the Bibliothèque
Nationale if they had had facilities for storing film; but anything to do with the CNC, after what they had done to him
in 1968, was out of the question.

"Langlois became more and more of a mythomaniac. It
may have been because of his declining health, but more than
ever before he refused to prepare coherently for the future. He
went more often to fortune-tellers, he sank deeper and deeper
into disorder: he was on a collision course."

Underneath the Arches

Or, as another friend put it, he didn't run away from his problems—he tried to *outrun* them: what the French call "*la fuite en avant.*" He had used this technique quite successfully in the past, and he couldn't stop: the Centre Pompidou (Beaubourg) had put a theater at Langlois's disposition, and although Langlois did not like the idea of Beaubourg or most of the people who were to run it, he wanted to put together as good a program as possible for the inauguration in the spring of 1977 of the new Cinémathèque theater.

13

The End

Henri Langlois died on January 12, 1977. His death was, to use one of his favorite phrases, surprising but not astonishing. The signs were all there, but most of us had refused to believe them. During the autumn of 1976, when he was in New York working hard, shut up in his hotel room on the American Cinematheque projects, he told Sallie Blumenthal that he was tired and that he would die within the year. He had said such things before, so none of his friends believed him.

The last time I saw him was during the Christmas holidays in 1976. I had just moved to Paris, and before going to Rome

The End

for a week in early January, I stopped at the Cinémathèque. He was suffering from an umbilical hernia; in spite of some intermittent efforts to lose weight, he was still enormous, and this exacerbated his other physical problems. Curiously, that last visit was the only time he ever called me by my first name. In all the eighteen years we had known each other, it was always "Roud." He used the familiar second person *tu*, but it was "Roud" and "Langlois" (whereas Mary Meerson insisted on the formal *vous* but called me Richard). At the time, I thought his calling me Richard was a little odd, but without any special significance. Later, of course, I wondered if he somehow knew we wouldn't be seeing each other again. . . .

I got the news of his death in Rome: Sallie Blumenthal phoned from New York because, as she said, she didn't want me to learn of it first from the newspapers. I was grateful, because the story did appear in all the newspapers in Rome.

The cause was given as heart failure. Sallie told me that it had happened late at night: he was working by candlelight at home. The electricity and phone had been cut off because he hadn't paid the bills. He was planning both the program for the Tours Film Festival and the programs for the new Cinémathèque theater at Beaubourg. (The work for the Tours festival was in part intended to bring in a little extra money so that he could pay his arrears to the government for the Social Security that employers are obliged to contribute for their employees.) With him was Peter Willits, a young Englishman who used to run a film society at Oxford University, and who was the last of Langlois's unpaid, devoted aides. Langlois was lying down with his foot swathed in cotton, socks, and blankets for his gout.

After a while, Willits and Langlois left Mary and their apartment and went next door to the flat of filmmakers Eila Hershon and Roberto Guerra, where there was a working telephone—and one of his last two calls was to Enno Patalas of the Munich Municipal Film Museum; the other was to Sallie Blumenthal in New York. He discussed some difficulties with the upcoming 1977 Metropolitan Museum show, and she remembers his repeating to her, in English: "Do not be afraid, do not be afraid." By two o'clock in the morning, he could do no more and said to Willits, "I've got to go to sleep." So they went next door to his and Mary Meerson's apartment. "He began to feel bad," says Willits, "going upstairs, and when we somehow got back to his bedroom, it was all over." He died, as it were, on the battlefield, and, as Willits puts it, "My last memory of him was of someone who killed himself working." He was in desperate need of money for the Cinémathèque, but to get it from the government would involve compromise on some level; he didn't want to get it from the film producers or companies because he was afraid they would lay hands on the Cinémathèque. He tried to get money the only way he could: by his own work. Sometimes, said Willits, they would work for forty-eight hours without stopping, completely cut off from the outside world.

The funeral was not held until the following week. Although Langlois had not been a practicing Roman Catholic, he had been baptized in that faith, and one of his best friends was Father Jean Diard, a Jesuit priest, who is very much interested in the cinema and the other arts. The funeral was held at St. Anne's, a church fairly near the Langlois home. I had expected to see all the New Wave directors who had benefited so much from the Cinémathèque and who had fought so hard to save Langlois's job in 1968. The church was crowded, but the only director I saw was Alain Resnais. Truffaut was in Hollywood at the time, and for whatever reason, neither Godard nor Chabrol, Rivette nor Rohmer, nor any of the others attended the funeral. Resnais's presence gave rise to a "gag" that Langlois would have loved. When I saw Resnais, we said hello, and I asked where his wife (Florence Malraux, daughter of André Malraux) was, since I didn't see her near him. "Oh, she's busy taking care of the tombstone," he said. "The tombstone?" I repeated. He saw the confused look on my face and hastily added, "Oh, no, not Langlois's tombstone, her father's." (Malraux had died in November 1976). Considering the complicated relationship between Langlois and Malraux, I had all I could do not to burst out laughing.

There were some well-known figures: Françoise Giroud, representing the government (she was Minister of Culture at the time), Simone Signoret, and Yves Montand. There were also many familiar faces to which I could not put a name: employees and ex-employees of the Cinémathèque. And of course, along with the official family—Langlois's brother Georges, his wife and children—there was Mary Meerson. Swathed in black from head to toe, she looked like a personage in Eisenstein's *Ivan the Terrible*: the image of grief. The ceremony was somewhat odd: Father Diard made the funeral address, but the only music was a flute solo by Debussy. The young man who played it reminded me of a scene in one of Langlois's favorite films, *Le Déjeuner sur l'Herbe* (*Picnic on the Grass*). It was somehow appropriate.

I didn't see him there, but Langlois's old archenemy Jacques Ledoux was present; Françoise Jaubert (daughter of the composer Maurice Jaubert, she had also worked with Henri at the Cinémathèque for a time back in the sixties) told me later that Ledoux went up to her and said, "Langlois was my father, too, just as much as he was yours."* After the

---

*In May 1977 at the FIAF Congress in Varna, Rumania, Jacques Ledoux said of Langlois: "Those who knew him are aware that he was a man excessive in every way, but fascinating because of those very excesses, an extraordinary melange of inspiration and preconceived ideas, of generosity and jealousy. He was at the origin of the creation of many *cinémathèques* (including the one I represent here), and I shall never forget that."

ceremony we went to the Montparnasse Cemetery (Jean Riboud paid for the funeral), where we found wreaths and crowns of flowers from archives all over the world. Although it was January, the sun was shining. Once the coffin was deposited in the grave, the group slowly began to disperse. Some went off to lunch—it had been a long morning; some went home. But everyone, I think, felt as I did—that we had lost a friend. We knew that the Cinémathèque would survive, which was all that Langlois cared about; we knew that the collection, in spite of all those notoriously rusty cans, would also survive. But even if the films had all turned immediately to dust, there would be a living memorial to Langlois in the work of those directors who had learned so much at the Cinémathèque.

But the man was gone and no one could replace him. There were many who thought—perhaps too pessimistically—that his life had embraced the history of the cinema. He was born in the year that the earliest great directors, Griffith and Feuillade, Stiller and Sjöström, had begun to do their first important work, and he died at a time when the great surge of talent that had started in the late fifties had, so it seemed, begun to lose momentum. It was not that these filmmakers would stop working or stop making good films, and in the sixties a large number of important directors had appeared all over the world. But by the mid-seventies, there seemed to be few new faces, few new talents.

Is the cinema dying? Quite possibly: there is no guarantee of eternal life for any art form. The heyday of opera, for example, lasted a bare two hundred years. But if the future of the cinema is in its past, that past has been preserved, largely through the efforts and the example of Henri Langlois.

Notes

Translations throughout this book are by Richard Roud unless credited otherwise.

INTRODUCTION

1. The comments quoted in the Introduction, unless otherwise cited, are from the film *Langlois* (1970) by Eila Hershon and Roberto Guerra.
2. *Cahiers du Cinéma*, No. 200–201 (April–May 1968).
3. Jean Narboni and Tom Milne, eds., *Godard on Godard*, trans. (London: Secker & Warburg, 1972; New York: The Viking Press, 1972).

Notes

CHAPTER 1

1. All quotations from the following persons are from taped conversations with the author, unless otherwise identified: Margareta Akermark, Kenneth Anger, Louise Brooks, Freddy Buache, Lotte Eisner, Marie Epstein, Georges Franju, Georges Goldfayn, S. Frederick Gronich, Thomas Johnston, Arthur Knight, Georges Langlois, Henri Langlois, Serge Losique, Bernard Martinand, Derek Prouse, Karel Reisz, Sheldon Renan, Alain Resnais, Jean Riboud, Jacques Rivette, David Robinson, Jean Rouch, Elliott Stein, André Thirifays, François Truffaut.
2. Cinémathèque program (Paris, 1955).
3. Cinémathèque program (Paris, 1956); reprinted in *Cahiers du Cinéma*, No. 200–201 (April–May 1968).
4. Ibid.

CHAPTER 2

1. *Études Cinématographiques*, Nos. 38–39 (Spring 1965).
2. Ibid.
3. *Regards*, No. 150 (November 26, 1936); reprinted in *Chroniques du Cinéma Français* (Paris: Union Générale des Éditions [1.0/1.8], 1979).
4. Ibid.
5. Ibid.

CHAPTER 3

1. *Remembering Iris Barry* (New York: Museum of Modern Art, 1980).
2. Interview with Jean-A. Gili, *Cinéma 71*, No. 153 (February 1971).

CHAPTER 4

1. Simone Signoret, *Nostalgia Isn't What It Used to Be* (New York: Harper and Row, 1978).

Notes

CHAPTER 5

1. *Cinéma* 69, No. 133 (June 1969).
2. *The New Yorker*, February 26, 1955.
3. Cinémathèque program (Paris, 1956); reprinted in *Cahiers du Cinéma*, No. 200–201 (April–May 1968).
4. *Cahiers du Cinéma*, No. 135 (September 1962).
5. Ibid.
6. Annette Insdorf, *François Truffaut* (Boston: Twayne Publishers, 1979).
7. *A History of the Cinema* (London, 1969; New York, 1978).
8. Narboni and Milne, eds., *Godard on Godard*. Tom Milne, co-editor and translator, identified the "anonymous French cameraman" as Felix Mesguisch.
9. Interview with Corine McMullin in *Vogue* (Paris), September 1974.
10. André Bazin, *What Is Cinema?*, trans. Hugh Gray (Berkeley: University of California Press, 1967).
11. *Sight and Sound*, April 1953.
12. *Film Culture*, April 1968.
13. *Cahiers du Cinéma*, No. 37 (July 1954).
14. *Cahiers du Cinéma*, No. 34 (April 1954).
15. *Cahiers du Cinéma*, No. 148 (October 1963).

CHAPTER 6

1. Dudley Andrew, *André Bazin* (New York: Oxford University Press, 1978).
2. *Film Comment*, March–April 1977.
3. Cinémathèque program (Paris, 1956).
4. Ibid.

CHAPTER 7

1. David Thomson, *Biographical Dictionary of the Cinema* (New York: William Morrow, 1976).
2. W. H. Auden, *The Dyer's Hand* (New York: Random House, 1963).

Notes

3. "Bodies in Space: Film as 'Carnal Knowledge,' " *Artforum*, February 1969.
4. Nestor Almendros, *Un Homme à la Camera* (Paris: Hatier, 1982).

CHAPTER 8

1. *Le Monde*, February 21, 1968.
2. Narboni and Milne, eds., *Godard on Godard*.
3. Report from Marc Allégret, April 1967.
4. Joseph McBride, *Focus on Film: Howard Hawks* (Englewood Cliffs, N.J.: Prentice-Hall, 1972).
5. *Sight and Sound*, July 1966.

CHAPTER 11

1. Interview with Edward Baron Turk, *American Film*, June 1980.
2. *Sight and Sound*, October 1972.
3. *Film Comment*, March–April 1977.

CHAPTER 12

1. Ada Louise Huxtable, *The New York Times*, April 13, 1973.
2. Ibid.

Index

Index

Index

Index

Index

Index